2nd Edition

Estate Planning Essentials

D1566989

by enodare publishing

Bibliographic data
- International Standard Book Number (ISBN): 978-1-906144-41-8
- Edition: Second Edition (2012)
- Printed in the United States of America
- First Printing: December 2010

Published by: Enodare Limited
                                  4747 36th Street
                                  Long Island City
                                  NY 11101, USA

Printed and distributed by: CreateSpace - An Amazon Company,
                                  On-Demand Publishing LLC
                                  Scotts Valley, CA 95066
                                  United States of America

For more information, e-mail books@enodare.com.

Trademarks

All terms mentioned in this book that are known to be trademarks or service
marks have been appropriately capitalized. Enodare cannot attest to the
accuracy of this information. Use of a term in this book should not be regarded
as affecting the validity of any trademark or service mark.

IMPORTANT NOTE

This book is meant as a general guide to estate planning. While considerable effort has been made to make this book as complete and accurate as possible, laws and their interpretation are constantly changing. As such, you are advised to update this information with your own research and/or counsel and to consult with your personal legal, financial and medical advisors before acting on any information contained in this book.

The purpose of this book is to educate and entertain. It is not meant to provide legal, financial or medical advice or to create any attorney-client or advisory relationship. The authors and publisher shall have neither liability (whether in negligence or otherwise) nor responsibility to any person or entity with respect to any loss or damage caused or alleged to be caused directly or indirectly by the information or documents contained in this book or the use of that information or those documents.

.

ABOUT ENODARE

Enodare, the international self-help legal publisher, was founded in 2000 by lawyers from one of the most prestigious international law firms in the World.

Our aim was simple - to provide access to quality legal information and products at an affordable price.

Our Will Writer software was first published in that year and, following its adaptation to cater for the legal systems of over 30 countries worldwide, quickly drew in excess of 40,000 visitors per month to our website. From this humble start, Enodare has quickly grown to become a leading international estate planning and asset protection self-help publisher with legal titles in the United States, Canada, the United Kingdom, Australia and Ireland.

Our publications provide customers with the confidence and knowledge to help them deal with everyday estate planning issues such as the preparation of a last will and testament, a living trust, a power of attorney, administering an estate and much more.

By providing customers with much needed information and forms, we enable them to place themselves in a position where they can protect both themselves and their families through the use of easy-to-read legal documents and forward planning techniques.

The Future....

We are always seeking to expand and improve the products and services we offer. However, in order to do this, we need to hear from interested authors and to receive feedback from our customers.

If something isn't clear to you in our publications, please let us know and we'll try to make it clearer in the next edition. If you can't find the answer you want and have a suggestion for an addition to our range, we'll happily look at that too.

USING SELF-HELP BOOKS

Before using a self-help book, you need to carefully consider the advantages and disadvantages of doing so – particularly where the subject matter is of a legal or tax related nature.

In writing our self-help books, we try to provide readers with an overview of the laws in a specific area. While this overview is often general in nature, it provides a good starting point for those wishing to carry out a more detailed review of a topic.

However, unlike an attorney advising a client, we cannot cover every conceivable eventuality that might affect our readers. Within the intended scope of this book, we can only cover the principal areas in a given topic and even where we cover these areas, we can still only do so to a moderate extent. To do otherwise would result in the writing of a text book which would be capable of use by legal professionals. This is not what we do.

We try to present useful information and documents that can be used by an average reader with little or no legal knowledge. While our sample documents can be used in the vast majority of cases, everybody's personal circumstances are different. As such, they may not be suitable for everyone. You may have personal circumstances which might impact the effectiveness of these documents or even your desire to use them. The reality is that without engaging an attorney to review your personal circumstances, this risk will always exist. It's for this very reason that you need to consider whether the cost of using a do-it-yourself legal document outweighs the risk that there may be something special about your particular circumstances which might not be taken into account by the sample documents attached to this book (or indeed any other sample documents).

It goes without saying (we hope) that if you are in any doubt as to whether the documents in this book are suitable for use in your particular circumstances, you should contact a suitably qualified attorney for advice before using them. Remember the decision to use these documents is yours! We are not advising you in any respect.

In using this book, you should also take into account the fact that this book has been written with the purpose of providing a general overview of the laws in the United States. As such, it does not attempt to cover all of the various procedural nuances and specific requirements that may apply from state to state – although we do point some of these out along the way.

Another thing that you should remember is that the law changes – thousands of new laws are brought into force every day and, by the same token, thousands are repealed or amended every day! As such, it is possible that while you are reading this book, the law might well have been changed. Let's hope it hasn't but the chance does exist! Needless to say, we take regular steps (including e-mail alerts) to update our customers about any changes to the law. We also ensure that our books are reviewed and revised regularly to take account of these changes.

Anyway, assuming that all of the above is acceptable to you, let's move on to exploring the topic at hand...........Estate Planning.

TABLE OF CONTENTS

AN INTRODUCTION TO ESTATE PLANNING

Despite the onslaught of estate planning books on to the market over the last number of years, many people remain only vaguely familiar with the subject. In fact, most still believe that estate planning is as simple as making a will. In some cases, this is correct, but often there is much more to it than that.

Estate planning may be described as the process of providing for the future management of your affairs should the time come when you are unable to do so yourself. It is also the means by which you arrange your affairs in a manner that will maximize the value of your estate passing to your desired beneficiaries following your death.

Important Note

The value of your estate at the time of your death will be equal to the value of your total assets - legal rights, interests and entitlements to property of any kind - less all your liabilities at that time.

In order to arrange your affairs, you may use devices such as wills, trusts, gifts, powers of attorney and living wills. This list is not exhaustive as many other devices exist through which you may transfer, protect and manage your estate. Through the use of these estate planning devices, you can determine:

- how and by whom your assets will be managed during any period in which you are incapacitated and unable to manage your affairs;

- how healthcare decisions will be made during any period in which you are incapacitated and unable to make such decisions yourself;

- when and under what circumstances your assets will be distributed during your lifetime; and

- how and to whom your assets will be distributed following your death.

The manner in which you choose to dispose of your estate is almost entirely up to you. Of course, in most cases your choices will be dictated by your personal circumstances and your priorities and preferences in life. For example, some of us are married, some divorced. Others have never been married. Some people have children and some do not. Some of us wish to leave everything to our children, and others, for one reason or another, do not wish for their children to inherit at all.

 Did Your Know!

By now, you've no doubt heard the story of Warren Buffet, the billionaire investor worth an estimated $37 billion in 2009, who announced in 2006 that he planned to give away much of his fortune to charity, with 83% of it allegedly going to the Bill & Melinda Gates Foundation. Or what about the multi-millionaire founder of The Body Shop, Dame Anita Roddick? She passed away in 2007 at the age of 64 leaving her entire estate to charity – leaving her two daughters without a single red cent on "moral grounds"!

Your unique circumstances and your beliefs are the very reasons why you must think and plan carefully about how you want your estate to be distributed after your death. If you do not make these decisions yourself, the law will make them for you!

In this book, we introduce you to some of the ways in which you can plan your estate. We will talk to you about wills, trusts, powers of attorneys, healthcare directives, beneficiaries, taxes and much more. We will get you thinking – and by the end of the process, you should have a solid understanding of estate planning and the techniques involved. If we are even luckier, we will have inspired you to actually make an estate plan. Indeed, people can and do prepare their own estate planning documents. In many cases, this can be done without the need for a lawyer. Of course, everyone's situation is different and sometimes you will need to get a lawyer involved. We will flag potentially tricky situations along the way and suggest to you that you may need some legal assistance in these areas.

For the moment, however, let us start by taking a brief look at what exactly estate planning is all about!

CHAPTER 1:
ESTATE PLANNING BASICS

Chapter Overview

In this chapter we will give you a brief introduction to estate planning and point out some of the reasons why everyone should plan their estate. We briefly discuss some of the specific issues that you may need to address and introduce you to the legal devices used to address these issues.

Chapter

1

CHAPTER 1

ESTATE PLANING BASICS

What Is Estate Planning?

As alluded to in the introduction, estate planning is the process of planning for the management of your estate in anticipation of your incapacity and the disposition of your assets upon death.

Preparing an estate plan is undoubtedly one of the most important steps that you can take in order to ensure that your healthcare wishes are honored should you become incapacitated, and that the your wishes regarding the transfer of your property on death are complied with.

While people traditionally believed that a will formed the pillar of a decent estate plan, more and more people now appreciate the value of a comprehensive estate plan. Such a plan includes relevant legal devices to transfer property, appoint guardians for children, reduce taxes, avoid probate, provide for the management of their financial affairs during times of incapacity and appoint agents to make healthcare decisions. A good estate plan should also contain details regarding funeral and burial arrangements. Irrespective of a person's age or the size of their estate, a good estate plan can accomplish each of these tasks.

For most people, understanding estate planning options can appear to be quite a demanding endeavor at first glance. However, as you will see later in this chapter, many of the estate planning techniques commonly used are relatively straightforward. We will explore some of these techniques in brief in the ensuing pages of this chapter before taking a more detailed look at these matters in later chapters.

What's Included in Your Estate?

So where do you start when you are making an estate plan? Well, before you decide who you want to give your assets to, you must first determine what assets you actually have to give away. In other words, you need to know what your estate is!

Simply put, your estate comprises of everything you own - all your property and possessions, including cash, investments, insurance policies, real estate, valuables, cars, jewelry and so on. It also includes any liabilities that you might have such as mortgages, car loans, outstanding utility bills, credit card bills and so on. The total value of your estate is equal to the "fair market value" of all of your various assets less all of your debts.

As we'll see later on in this book, the value of your estate is important when it comes to determining whether your estate will be liable to pay any estate taxes after your death.

How to Plan Your Estate

Once you know exactly what you have to give away, you will need to look at the various estate planning options that are available to and suitable for you. Fortunately, estate planning is not as difficult or as complicated as it is often made out to be. In most cases, it simply involves a detailed consideration of your situation in life and how you would like your affairs managed if you become incapacitated or how you would want your assets distributed in the unfortunate event of your death. Once you understand the options available to you, you should be able to answer these questions a lot easier. At that stage, you can use a number of devices and legal documents to put your estate plan in to effect.

Surprisingly, preparing the legal documents is often the easiest part of the process. The most difficult part for most people is actually deciding on what they want to include in their plan. This is because there are a variety of different issues to consider before finalizing your plan. At the very least, you must ask yourself (and illicit answers for) the following questions:

- what assets do I own and how much are they worth?

- how much debt do I have?

- whom do I want to give my assets to when I pass away?

- do I want to wait until I die before giving my assets away or would it be better if I did it sooner?

- who should I appoint to manage my assets if I am unable to do so due to ill health?

- who should I appoint to take care of my minor children if I become unable to care for them myself?

- who should make medical decisions on my behalf if I become unable to do so?

Of course, there are many other questions that can and should be asked. However, for the moment the questions above are probably enough to get you started on your journey to preparing your estate plan.

Do I Need to Plan My Estate?

Many people often think estate planning is for the wealthy or simply believe that there is no need for them to have an estate plan – after all, they don't have much anyway. The reality is that anyone who has reached the age of majority in their state, has any assets which are important to them, or who has children should make an estate plan.

The fact is, whether your estate is large or small, there are many compelling reasons why everyone (with very few exceptions) should take the time to organize and plan their estate. For example, developing and implementing a good estate plan will ensure:

- that your assets will be managed during any period in which you are incapacitated;

- that someone you know and trust will be able to make medical decisions on your behalf in accordance with your specific instructions and wishes should you become incapacitated;

- that your assets will be disposed of as you would have wanted following your death;

- that your family and friends will not have to wait months or even years to receive their inheritance following your death;

- that your children will be properly looked after by a guardian of your choosing and not one appointed by a court; and

- much more.

When it comes to estate planning, one thing is certain. If you fail to plan ahead, a judge will make all of the above decisions for you. In making these decisions, the judge will look at your state's law and the predefined estate plan that applies for everyone who fails to plan for the distribution of their estate themselves. In essence, a court will appoint someone to make medical decisions on your behalf, dictate who receives your assets based on specific rules of inheritance (known as the rules of intestacy), appoint someone to look after your children and much more. What is worse, neither your wishes nor those of your family can override the decision of the court.

From the above, you can see that one of the most compelling reasons to prepare an estate plan sooner rather than later is control. If you have a proper estate plan in place then you, and not a court, can determine how your affairs are dealt with.

We will now take a brief introductory look at some of the various estate planning devices and techniques that you may need to use to implement your plan once you have finalised your thoughts in that respect.

Children and Guardians

If you are a parent, it is likely that your first priority will be to make proper arrangements for the future care of your children should you and your spouse or partner die before they grow up. You can do this by simply appointing a guardian who will be responsible for their care, welfare and education. A guardian can be appointed under the terms of a specific guardianship agreement or under the terms of your will.

Remember, if you fail to appoint a guardian for your children, the court will appoint one of its choosing. On the other hand, if you plan your estate in advance, you can be sure your children are well taken care of by people you know and trust.

Apart from the day-to-day care of your children, you will also need to consider who will have day-to-day responsibility for managing any inheritances they receive whether from you or from someone else. As we will see in the next chapter, in many states, minor children are not allowed to own significant property or assets outright. As a result, it becomes necessary to appoint a property guardian or trustee to manage those assets on their behalf. A property guardian or trustee (while similar to each other) is different to a personal guardian in that they are only concerned with the management of the child's property and not specifically with the child's care, welfare or education. This remains the responsibility of the personal guardian. Often, the same person is appointed as personal guardian, property guardian and trustee. However, you may wish to separate the tasks, as many do, and assign them to those people you feel best qualify for the particular job in question.

For more information on children, guardianship and property management options for children please see Chapter 2.

Choosing Beneficiaries

Deciding on who will be entitled to receive your assets following your death can be an extremely rewarding and gratifying experience.

While many people simply choose to leave their estate to their spouse or children, the exact decision as to who will benefit from your estate and the manner in which your estate will pass to those beneficiaries will most likely be influenced by a number of important factors including whether:

- your intended beneficiaries are minors or adults? If they are children, you will most likely need to make arrangements to have someone manage their inheritance until they reach a specific age;

- you have any children with special needs? If so, you may wish to create a trust to provide for their long-term care?

- your beneficiary, irrespective of his or her age, is sufficiently capable of managing a large inheritance on his or her own or whether they need assistance? Again a trust may be considered;

- you wish to disinherit your spouse or child? If you do, there are only a limited number of ways in which you can do this! We'll look at this further in later chapters;

- you want to leave something to charity? If so, you could use tax efficient trusts to leave these gifts. We discuss these in later chapters; and

- there will be tax implications associated with the giving of assets to a particular beneficiary? Again, tax can be deferred or, in some cases, avoided by the use of specific devices.

All of the above considerations, and more, will play a fundamental part in your choice as to who receives your specific assets and the manner in which they do so. We will discuss these matters in further detail later in this book.

For more information on beneficiaries, please see Chapter 3.

Last Will and Testament

A will, more formally known as a "last will and testament", is a legal document that allows you to express your desires and intentions with regard to the transfer of your real and personal property following your death. It allows you to put your wishes down "for the record" so that, should disputes or confusion arise, you may be assured that your intentions will be respected and followed after your death. Both statutory and common law (laws as interpreted by the courts) require that your heirs follow your documented wishes when determining how your estate is divided amongst them.

For those with sizeable estates, a will can play a strategic role in tax planning. The manner in which your property is passed, how much of it is passed and to whom it is passed determines how both the estate and the recipients of such property are taxed. A carefully drafted will can reduce estate and inheritance taxes, transfer costs and even the general costs of probate and administration.

Apart from prescribing how your property should be transferred to your loved ones following your death, a will is extremely flexible when it comes to managing property transferred to children. You can choose from a variety of property management options for children who are to receive property under your will. In addition, your will also affords you the opportunity to choose a personal guardian to care for your minor children after your death.

The terms of your will also usually dictate who will look after your affairs and take charge of carrying out your instructions following your death, including your sentimental, burial and memorial wishes. This of course is important as you will invariably want to ensure that the person managing your affairs (ie. your executor) will honor the various choices that you have made in your will.

The primary drawback of using a will is that it can take a number of months (and sometimes years) to complete the probate process – the formal process by which assets are transferred to the beneficiaries named in a will. This process often has the effect of slowing down the transfer of many of the estate's assets to the intended beneficiaries. To avoid this problem, there are numerous estate planning tools that can be utilized and we will discuss each of these further below.

For more information on wills, please see Chapter 4.

Revocable Living Trusts

A revocable living trust is a type of 'inter vivos' trust (i.e. a trust made between living people) used for estate planning purposes. Under the living trust arrangement you, as the creator of the trust, declare yourself trustee of the trust and then transfer some or all of your personal property to the trust. The legal ownership of the property passes from you personally to the trust. However, as trustee of the trust you maintain control over and use of the trust property.

As creator of the living trust, you can, at any time, either revoke the trust or call for the return of some or all of the property transferred to it. You can also add assets to the trust, change the terms of the trust and even make it irrevocable (incapable of change) at any time in the future.

After your death, the trust assets will pass to the beneficiaries that you have named in the trust document in much the same way that they would under a will. Specifically, your trust document will nominate a person known as the "successor trustee" (which is a little like an executor or personal representative) who will have the responsibility of transferring ownership of the assets in the trust to the beneficiaries named in the trust document following your death. In most cases, the whole transfer process takes only a few weeks.

From an estate planning perspective, one of the most important features to note is that since the assets in the trust are legally owned by the trust, they will not form part of your probatable estate at the time of your death. As such, there will be no need for any of these assets to go through the probate process; nor may those assets be available to settle debts from your estate (other than taxes which might be due). This, in turn, allows for the speedy distribution of those assets to the beneficiaries named in the trust document. Once all of the assets are transferred to the beneficiaries, the living trust ceases to exist.

Revocable living trusts are very easy to establish and manage and, apart from avoiding probate, there are many advantages to using living trusts as part of your overall estate plan. These reasons relate to the management of your assets during incapacity, privacy, tax and more.

For more information on revocable living trusts, please see Chapter 9.

Executors and Probate

As briefly mentioned above, probate is the court supervised administrative process by which the assets of a deceased person are gathered, applied to pay debts, taxes and expenses of administration and then distributed to the beneficiaries named in the deceased's will. This process generally takes six to twelve months to complete, but where complexities arise it can last for years! In most cases, assets cannot or at least should not be transferred to the beneficiaries under the will until probate has been completed.

It follows, therefore, that where you make a will, you will also need to appoint an executor (otherwise known as a personal representative) to probate your estate following your death. Your executor will be responsible for handling, safeguarding and distributing your property in accordance with the terms of your will. In addition, he or she will also be responsible for ensuring that any debts or taxes owing by you at the date of your death are paid by your estate. These payments, if any, are often paid from the assets of the estate before any distributions are made to the beneficiaries named in a will.

For more information on executors and probate, please see Chapter 5.

Assets that Don't Go Through Probate

If you have a spouse, child or other person that is financially dependent on you, they may need immediate access to funds from your estate in the event of your death. As such, you will need to consider how you can transfer some or all of your assets to them in a manner that will avoid a potentially long probate process.

This can be achieved in a number of ways. Firstly, you can avail of some of the probate free transfer devices such as pay on death bank accounts, transfer on death securities or even life policies with designated beneficiaries. In each case, you can nominate a beneficiary for the proceeds of the account/policy and the financial institution holding same will quickly arrange the transfer of the proceeds to the named beneficiary upon production of your death certificate. These methods provide a great source of readily available funds following your death.

Secondly, you could transfer your assets to a living trust. Assets held in a living trust will not become part of your probatable estate because the assets are not held in your name. This allows them to be quickly distributed to the beneficiaries of the trust following your death.

Thirdly, you can convert assets that you own solely into jointly owned assets. Where assets are jointly owned, it is possible to designate that a right of survivorship will apply to these assets. This means that when one of the joint owners die, the asset will pass directly to the surviving joint owner – without the need for probate. Of course, the joint owner can be a friend or relative; and the assets can comprise of anything from real estate to cash in a bank account. Thus, in the same way as the other devices mentioned above, the surviving joint owner can quickly claim ownership of the asset following your death by simply producing a certified copy of your death certificate.

For more information on assets that don't go through probate, please see Chapter 8.

Planning for Incapacity – Power of Attorney for Finance and Property

A power of attorney is a legal document by which you appoint and authorize another person (usually a trusted friend, family member, colleague or adviser) to act on your behalf in the event that you become incapacitated.

In order for a power of attorney to apply when you are incapacitated, it will need to be stated to be a durable power of attorney. Ordinary powers of attorney cease to have legal effect once you become incapacitated. A durable power of attorney remains valid or, in some cases, only commences if you become incapacitated.

Durable powers of attorney come in two forms – a durable general power of attorney and a durable limited power of attorney. Under a durable general power of attorney, you can appoint an agent to whom you give authority to collect and disburse money on your behalf; operate your bank accounts; buy and sell property in your name; refurbish and rent out your property; and generally sign documents and deeds as your *alter ego*. It permits your agent to act as your authorized legal representative in relation to the whole cross-section of your legal and financial affairs, until such time as the authorization granted under the power of attorney is revoked or comes to an end.

You can of course limit the scope of your agent's authority by creating a durable limited power of attorney. This is similar to a durable general power of attorney except that, under the terms of this document, you can expressly limit the agent's authority to carrying out certain functions such as, for example, the management of your business, selling a property or another specific task.

Most responsible individuals plan how their property will be divided amongst their loved ones following their death. However, all of these plans can seem like a waste of time and effort if the individual, through an accident or illness, finds themselves in a position where they cannot manage their own affairs while they are still alive. The individual's inability to manage his or her own assets, in particular, could result in a substantial depletion of the value of those assets. This could, in turn, render meaningless the individual's plans for the distribution of his or her assets on death.

The individual's family could be left facing serious financial hardship due to their inability to access the individual's assets while he or she is still alive. What if the individual's signature is required to access the family savings? What if assets need to be sold to pay for his or her medical care…but because he or she cannot sign the relevant documents, the family cannot raise the funds.

You can avoid this situation entirely by simply granting a durable power of attorney to a close friend or family member. If the need arises, they can take charge of your affairs and ensure that they are managed in much the same way as you would have done in the circumstances.

For more information on powers of attorney for finance and property, please see Chapter 6.

Planning for Incapacity – Advance Healthcare Directives

Advance healthcares directives are used to instruct others regarding the medical care that you would like to receive should you find yourself in a position where you cannot communicate your own wishes regarding same.

There are two specific types of healthcare directive that should be considered as part of your estate plan, each with differing features. These are living wills and healthcare powers of attorney.

Living Wills

A living will is a legal document by which you can instruct healthcare providers with regard to your wishes about the use or non-use of certain life-prolonging medical procedures, in the event that you become terminally ill or permanently unconscious and unable to communicate your wishes.

For many, the purpose of a living will is to document their wish that life-sustaining treatment, including artificially or technologically supplied nutrition and hydration, be withheld or withdrawn if they are unable to make medical decisions on their own behalf and are suffering from a terminal illness or are in a permanent state of unconsciousness from which they are unlikely to recover.

The manner in which a living will works is quite straightforward. In most states, two doctors must personally examine you and agree that medical procedures will only prolong the dying process. If both doctors agree that this is the case, then certain medical procedures may be withdrawn or withheld, depending on the contents of your living will. Of course, the withdrawal of these procedures will result in death. However, it should be noted that living wills can also be used to instruct attending physicians to use all possible means and treatments to keep you alive.

Other names sometimes found for living wills include 'instructions', 'directive to physicians', 'declaration' and 'advance medical directive'.

Healthcare Powers of Attorney

One of the principal limitations of living wills is that they come into play only when you are either terminally ill or permanently unconscious and can't specifically tell your doctors what you want done. Moreover, they also only deal with the receipt or non-receipt of life sustaining treatments. They would not, for example, apply where you were temporarily unconscious due to a relatively minor accident.

Whereas with a healthcare power of attorney, you can appoint a person you know and trust to make and communicate decisions on the receipt or non-receipt of all forms of medical treatment on your behalf. You don't even have to be terminally ill or permanently unconscious. You simply need to be unable to communicate your healthcare preferences. When this occurs, your appointed agent is entitled to step up and make medical decisions on your behalf.

This authority is effective only when your attending physician determines that you have lost the capacity to make informed healthcare decisions for yourself. As long as you still have this capacity, you retain the right to make all medical and other healthcare decisions on your behalf.

In your healthcare power of attorney, you may also limit the healthcare decisions that your agent will have authority to make. The authority of your agent to make healthcare decisions for you will generally include the authority to give informed consent; refuse to give informed consent; or to withdraw informed consent for any care, treatment, service or procedure designed to maintain, diagnose, or treat a physical or mental condition.

For more information on advanced healthcare directives, please see Chapter 7.

Reducing Taxes on Your Estate

A good estate plan will be structured in the most tax efficient manner to ensure that your estate pays as little in estate taxes as possible. Every amount paid in taxes is ultimately deducted from the amount payable from your estate to your loved ones. As such, it's very important, particularly where you have a valuable estate, that you seek tax advice when preparing your estate plan and that you utilize as many of the available tax planning opportunities as possible.

For more information on reducing taxes, please see Chapter 10.

Funeral Arrangements

Every good estate plan should encompass a funeral plan yet, despite all the obvious advantages, most people die without any form of pre-arranged plan.

If you make your wishes known in advance, you can make sure that there is no doubt or confusion among those who are close to you as to what you would like as your final tribute. These are choices that should be only yours and it is wise to prepare them in advance.

There are a number of benefits to making a funeral plan including:

- peace of mind - plan ahead so you can help to relieve loved ones of the future worry, uncertainty and expense;

- you can specify if you would like burial or cremation;

- you can decide on your final resting place;

- you can make others aware of arrangements you have already made; and

- you can specify your wishes for the type of service you would like.

Resource

For further information on funeral planning, see our book entitled "Funeral Planning Basics - a Step-By-Step Guide to Funeral Planning". See page 267

Conclusion

As you may have gathered, there are numerous benefits and satisfactions that can be derived from a good estate plan including:

- the provision of care and welfare of your immediate family;

- the transfer of property to your beneficiaries as quickly and inexpensively as possible;

- the reduction of taxes on your estate, and the resulting increase in the value of the gifts you make to your beneficiaries;

- the ability to choose the right executors and trustees for your estate;

- the minimizing of strain and uncertainty for your family;

- the pleasure of helping a favorite cause;

- the ability to manage the inheritances of family members/friends who need help and guidance with the management of their own affairs; and

- the avoidance of probate on your estate altogether!

In estate planning, money is not the root of all evil; it is procrastination that presents the real danger. If you procrastinate for too long and put off planning your estate, it becomes very unlikely that your property will be distributed entirely as you would have wished. However, it also becomes very likely that your family and friends will suffer personally and financially. So don't procrastinate – take some simple steps to begin the process of creating your estate plan!

CHAPTER 2:

CHILDREN, GUARDIANS AND PROPERTY MANAGEMENT

Chapter Overview

A guardian is a person appointed to have the legal authority (and the corresponding duty) to care for the personal and property interests of another person, usually children or other dependents. Most countries and states have laws that provide that the parents of a minor child are the legal guardians of that child, and that the parents can designate who shall become the child's legal guardian in the event of their death. The following chapter provides an overview and suggestions for choosing a guardian and for providing for the management of property left to children.

CHAPTER 2

CHILDREN, GUARDIANS AND PROPERTY MANAGEMENT

What Is a Guardian?

A guardian is the person responsible for a child's (or other dependent or incapacitated person's) physical care, education, health and welfare; as well as for making decisions about the child's faith-related matters. In some states, a non-parent guardian is called a 'conservator'.

In the normal scheme of things, if you are married and have a child you and your spouse are the primary legal guardians of your minor children, including any children that you may have adopted together. If you pass away, then your surviving spouse becomes the sole guardian of these children. However, should your surviving spouse also pass away, and neither of you have made any provisions for the appointment of a guardian then the children could become the responsibility of the court. Where this happens, there is a real risk that your children will end up being cared for by people that you would never have wished to raise them.

If you have children, it is therefore vital to plan ahead and ensure that they will be properly cared for in the event that neither you nor your spouse are around to do so. In this respect, you should give careful thought and consideration to naming a guardian and an alternate guardian in your will to take care of your children following your passing.

Sole and Joint Guardians

You have the option of appointing one or more guardians to care for your children. If you appoint one guardian, he or she will be known as a "sole guardian" and will be solely responsible for the welfare of your children and for making all decisions on their behalf. Alternatively, you can also nominate two or more people to serve as joint-guardians to the children. However, with joint guardians, each of them must reach agreement in relation to decisions regarding the children in their care. It is for this reason that joint-guardians are usually only nominated where they are married to each other or live together, as well as where they each have an important relationship to the children (uncles or aunts, for example).

If you are considering appointing a married couple as joint-guardians of your children, be sure to carefully consider the status of the couple's relationship and whether you would want both spouses to serve as guardians if they were ever separated or divorced. In such instances, it may be preferable to simply appoint one spouse as guardian at the very outset. The choice, however, is yours.

Alternate Guardians

When appointing a guardian, it is generally recommended that you also appoint an alternate guardian (or several alternates, hierarchically) who will serve if, for any reason, your first named guardian (known as your 'primary guardian') is unable or unwilling to serve when the time comes. If your first choice guardian cannot serve and you fail to name an alternate guardian in your will, it will then fall for the court to step in and determine who will act as guardian to your children. As alluded to above, the court's appointee may not be someone that you would have approved of had you the opportunity to do so!

As with your choice of primary guardians, you may also nominate an alternate guardian to serve alone or name two or more to serve jointly with each other.

Remember - your choice of alternate guardian is every bit as important as your choice of primary guardian!

Appointment of a Guardian

In most cases, a guardian can be appointed under the terms of your will by simply adding a standard guardianship clause. This will go some way towards ensuring that your children are cared for by someone who shares your values and ideals and who will properly care for the children. However, simply nominating a person to act as a guardian under your will is by no means absolute. It does not guarantee that your nominee will automatically become the permanent or legal guardian of your children. The final say as to whether a person nominated as a guardian under a will should be permitted to become the legal guardian of the children in question rests with a judge in the state where your children reside. For this very reason, it is often recommended that, in nominating a person to act as a guardian to your children, you also explain the rationale for the nomination and, in particular, why you believe the nominee would be most suitable for the role. These types of explanations can have a significant impact on the court's approval of your nominee.

 Did You Know?

It is also possible to appoint guardians by written agreement with the guardian.

You may also nominate different guardians to look after different interests of your children, e.g. financial, educational, spiritual, etc. In this way, you can choose to give your children the best part of each of your guardians.

Who Can Be a Guardian?

Well, the short answer is that anyone can be a guardian provided that they are agreeable to acting as a guardian to your children and are themselves an adult.

Should You Appoint Guardians for Your Minor Children?

Absolutely! If you have children under the age of majority in your state then you should appoint a responsible guardian to take care of them should it be necessary.

The age of majority for each state is set out in the table below.

Age of Majority in the United States	
Age 18	Alaska, Arizona, California, Colorado, Connecticut, District of Columbia, Florida, Georgia, Hawaii, Idaho, Illinois, Indiana, Iowa, Kansas, Kentucky, Louisiana, Maine, Maryland, Massachusetts, Michigan, Minnesota, Missouri, Montana, New Hampshire, New Mexico, New Jersey, New York, North Carolina, North Dakota, Oklahoma, Oregon, Pennsylvania, Rhode Island, South Carolina, South Dakota, Texas, Vermont, Washington, West Virginia and Wyoming.
Age 19	Alabama, Delaware and Nebraska.
Age 21	Mississippi.
Graduation or 18 - (whichever occurs first)	Ohio and Utah.
Graduation or 18 (whichever occurs later)	Arkansas, Tennessee and Virginia.
Graduation or 18 – (whichever occurs first) or 19 if still at school	Nevada and Wisconsin.

What to Consider When Choosing a Guardian for Your Child

As you will be leaving the responsibility of caring for your children to another person, the decision as to whom you should appoint as a guardian to your children is an extremely important one; and one that should not be made lightly. You will need to take many factors into consideration. Ultimately, however, you should choose the person you believe will offer the best care and support to your children. Often this will be a close relative or family friend. However, before actually appointing them as guardian under your will, it is very important that you check with your proposed nominee to ensure that he or she is willing to accept such a responsible and onerous role. There is no point in nominating someone if you think they will refuse to accept the role when the time comes.

Important Tip

Discuss your choice of guardian with the person(s) you have selected and make sure he or she (or they) is (are) willing to accept the responsibility should it become necessary.

There are many things that you will need to take into account when considering whether a person would be the right person to appoint as a guardian to your children. In particular, you should ask yourself the following questions regarding the proposed nominee:

- is the person you are considering willing to accept the long-term responsibility of being a guardian to your children? If the person is not willing or is not fully committed, you need to consider someone else;

- is this person responsible and up to the task of raising your children?

- is the person an adult? Remember, a minor cannot act as a legal guardian for another minor!

- where does this person reside?

- would your children be uprooted and moved away from their friends and family members if they went to live with this guardian? Would that be in their best interests?

- if you have more than one child, do you want your children to remain together? If you do then be sure to name the same guardian for all of your children. Note: judges are often wary of separating siblings and they do have the ultimate say in the matter;

- what is this person's home situation? For example, does he or she have a house or a one-bed apartment? Is the potential guardian in a stable relationship?

- will the potential guardian be able to provide your children with a stable positive environment and home life?

- will your children still have easy access to their other relatives – such as grandparents?

- what are the person's religious and moral beliefs?

- does the person have any medical conditions or other issues that would prevent them from being a suitable guardian?

- if you cannot make sufficient provision for your children's long-term care, will this person be able to afford to care for your children?

These are all very important and relative questions, but only the tip of the iceberg.

Once you have selected someone to act as a guardian to your children, it is important to discuss the potential appointment with him or her (or them) in detail. While most people are flattered, you will find that some are unable or unwilling to accept the responsibility. Be wary also of people agreeing to accept the role insincerely in the expectation that they will never be called upon to act. This is another very good reason to appoint an alternate guardian - just in case thr primary guardian is unable or unwilling to assume the role when the time comes.

Again, we must stress that naming a person as guardian in a will is merely a nomination, not the actual appointment (even though the word "appoint" will often be used in the guardian clause of a will). A court will still need to approve the appointment of the guardian you nominated. In the normal course, the court will usually ratify the appointment of a person nominated in a will. However, it is always possible that interested family members or other parties may challenge the appointment. Were this to happen, the court would listen to all relevant parties before making a determination as to whether the nomination should stand or whether it would be in the best interests of the children to have another person appointed as guardian. Usually, the court will appoint the person nominated in the will unless it finds compelling reasons not to do so. The court is concerned primarily with the best interests of the children.

Given the requirement for court approval and the potential of challenge, it is important that you specify, either in your will or on a separate document, the reasons for appointing the guardian in question. This will have a strong persuasive effect when being considered by the court.

If you are not married to the other parent of your minor child, it is important to understand that the nomination of a guardian in your will does not of itself grant priority to your guardian over the rights of the surviving parent if you die. In most cases, the surviving parent's rights will take priority over the rights of your nominated guardian.

What Happens When No Guardian Is Named in Your Will?

If you don't name a guardian for your children under the terms of your will, or elsewhere in a legal document, then the courts will decide who is best placed to act as their guardian. The courts usually give preference to family members based on the family member's relationship to the children. In most cases, if available and willing, the children's other parent is the automatic first choice to care for them. However, if the other parent is unwilling or unable to act, the courts will look at other family members.

In circumstances where you are separated or divorced, or where you are essentially a single parent, you may not want your child's other parent to have custody or guardianship rights over your child. This may be because you feel that the other parent is incapable or will not properly care for your child. You may feel that the other parent has effectively abandoned your child which therefore makes them an illogical choice for guardian. If you anticipate that such a situation may arise, contact an attorney or legal aid service as they will be able to advise you appropriately and may even draft a pre-emptive guardianship agreement for your child that, hopefully, the court will later approve. You will also want to document your reasons for wishing the other parent to remain out of the picture. At times, a court will grant custody to someone other than a surviving parent if it is satisfied that the surviving parent has legally abandoned the child (by not providing for or visiting that child for an extended period of time) or that the surviving parent is unfit or unsuitable to properly care for the child.

Where the other parent is not available or deemed to be unsuitable, the court will look next to the child's grandparents, aunts or uncles, adult siblings or other relatives to see if they would be a suitable guardian. Remember, however, that a court will not know your children or your wishes for them. As such, if you believe that any of these relatives would be unsuitable (for whatever reason) you should visit your attorney with a view to making legal arrangements for someone else to care for your child.

 Important Tip

If you are concerned that a relative might legally challenge your decision about your choice of guardian for your children, we recommend that you contact a suitably qualified attorney to discuss your situation.

Management of Children's Property

While the appointment of a guardian to care for and to raise your child is important, it is equally important to consider who will manage the money and property your child inherits from you; and indeed from anyone else. As mentioned earlier, children who have not yet reached the age of majority lack sufficient legal capacity to receive and manage inherited property. While this lack of capacity is often not an issue for most minors, it is problematic where they inherit significant or valuable assets. In such cases, it will be necessary to appoint an adult called a 'custodian', 'trustee' or 'property guardian' to receive and manage the property on behalf of the minor.

If you don't make arrangements to provide for the future management of your children's property, the court will do it for you by appointing a 'property guardian' of its choosing to manage the inheritances. Similar to the situation with normal guardians, a court will often appoint the surviving parent but this is not always the case. A third party or court appointed guardian can be appointed to deal with the property and, in such cases, that property guardian will have complete control over your children's inheritance. As such, it is important that you deal with this appointment in your will or in another legal agreement.

Options for Property Management

Fortunately, it is relatively easy and straightforward to avoid the uncertainties and hassles of a court-appointed guardianship. You can choose someone now to manage any property that your minor or young adult children may someday inherit from you. While there are many ways that you can structure this arrangement, four of the simplest and most commonly used methods are listed below.

Appointment of a Property Guardian

A property guardian is a person you appoint to be responsible for managing the property you leave to your children plus any other property that your children might receive. A property guardian is bound to manage the property in your children's best interests, using it to pay for normal living expenses, as well as health and educational needs.

If you name a property guardian for your children in your will, when the time comes, the court will (in the absence of strong reasons to do otherwise) formally appoint your selected person as property guardian to your children.

While a property guardian is appointed under the terms of your will, the scope of his or her management authority extends beyond the management of property left to your children under your will. In fact, it extends to include any property later received by your children where there are no pre-existing arrangements for management of that property (such as under a trust). As such, should your children receive an inheritance from a long lost relative, their property guardian is authorized to manage that property in the absence of your relative having provided for a specific means of management.

Remember, a property guardian is different to a personal guardian; the latter guardian is responsible for the care, health, welfare and education of the child. A property guardian is only responsible for managing the child's property – although he or she can apply the managed property for the benefit of the child's care, health, welfare or education. Do not make the mistake of appointing only a property guardian and thinking that he or she will also be responsible for the day-to-day care of the child!

Uniform Transfer to Minors' Act

As often mentioned, minors in most states do not have the legal capacity to enter into certain legal contracts, and are therefore not in position where they can own and manage assets such as stocks, bonds, funds, life insurance receipts and other annuities. It is therefore important to recognize that you cannot simply transfer any of these types of items directly to your minor children; or indeed to any other minor.

One of the most common methods used to get around this problem comes in the form of a custodianship created under either the Uniform Gift to Minors Act ("UGMA") or the Uniform Transfer to Minors Act ("UTMA"). Rather than transferring assets directly to your children on your death, you transfer your assets to a custodian who will hold those assets on trust for your children until they reach a pre-determined age. Once your children reach this age, the custodian will transfer the property that he or she is holding on their behalf to them. In the interim period, the custodian will be obliged to manage the property on your children's behalf in accordance with the provisions set out in the UGMA/UTMA.

The UGMA, which was enacted before the UTMA, created a very simple way for assets to be transferred to children under a trust arrangement without the need for lawyers and without the associated legal costs. To set up a custodianship under the UGMA, all a person needed to do was identify the property which he or she wished to transfer to a child (it can be any child named under a will or trust – not just the child of the testator or grantor) and to name a custodian to manage that property in the event that the child in question had not reached a designated age (usually between 18 to 25 years depending on state law) at the time they became entitled to receive the gift.

A typical clause of this type would be as follows:-

"I give $25,000 to James Jones, as custodian for Sarah Parker under the California Uniform Transfers to Minors Act, to hold until Sarah Parker reaches the age of 21 years."

While the UTMA is similar in its approach to the UGMA, it is widely considered to be more flexible than the UGMA, which was repealed to a large degree by the UTMA. While the UTMA affords minors much of the same benefits as the previous act, it also allows minors to own other types of property (apart from cash) such as real estate, patents and royalties and more importantly, for the transfers to occur through inheritance and not simply by means of a gift.

The UTMA have been adopted in all states except for Vermont and South Carolina.

The age at which the custodianship terminates is the age at which a minor becomes legally entitled to call for the assets held by a custodian to be transferred to him or her, and to have the custodial trust terminated. The table below shows the ages of termination of custodianships in the various states which have adopted the UTMA. As you will see, the ages vary from 18 to 25 years of age. You will also see that in some states the age is specified, while in other states a range of ages is provided from which the will or trust maker can chose a particular age.

You should be aware that the age of termination of a custodianship is not necessarily the same as the age of majority in a particular state.

AGE LIMITS FOR PROPERTY MANAGEMENT IN UTMA STATES			
State	Age at Which Minor Gets Property	State	Age at Which Minor Gets Property
Alabama	21	Missouri	21
Alaska	18 to 25	Montana	21
Arizona	21	Nebraska	21
Arkansas	18 to 21	Nevada	18 to 25
California	18 to 25	New Hampshire	21
Colorado	21	New Jersey	18 to 21
Connecticut	21	New Mexico	21
Delaware	21	New York	21
District of Columbia	18 to 21	North Carolina	18 to 21
Florida	21	North Dakota	21
Georgia	21	Ohio	18 to 21
Hawaii	21	Oklahoma	18 to 21
Idaho	21	Oregon	21 to 25
Illinois	21	Pennsylvania	21 to 25
Indiana	21	Rhode Island	21
Iowa	21	South Dakota	18
Kansas	21	Tennessee	21 to 25
Kentucky	18	Texas	21
Maine	18 to 21	Utah	21
Maryland	21	Virginia	18 to 21
Massachusetts	21	Washington	21
Michigan	18 to 21	West Virginia	21
Minnesota	21	Wisconsin	21
Mississippi	21	Wyoming	21

Individual Child Trusts

A child's trust is valid in all U.S. states and can be created under the terms of a will (such trusts are often called testamentary trust) or a living trust (such trusts are known as child sub-trusts).

A trust is a fiduciary arrangement whereby a person is appointed to become the legal owner of trust property, which they will hold for the benefit of another person. A child trust is a trust created for the benefit of a child. You can create a separate child trust for each of your children (if you wish) and for any other minor who stands to inherit under the terms of your will or living trust.

In your will or living trust document, you can name a trustee (usually a trusted relative or friend) who will manage the inheritance that a child will receive (as a beneficiary of that trust) until that child reaches an age specified by you. If the child in question has reached that age at the time of your death, and is past the age of majority for their state, the trust never actually comes into existence and the property is instead transferred directly to them upon your death.

However, where your child is under the age specified in your will or trust document, the inheritance will be transferred to a separate trust fund and will be managed by the nominated trustee in accordance with provisions set out in your will or trust document. The trustee will continue to manage the trust property until the child in question has reached the age specified in your will or trust document. At that time, the remainder of the trust property will be transferred to the now adult beneficiary and the trust will be terminated.

During the course of the trust, the trustee will have broad discretion over the management and distribution of the trust property. If the trustee deems it appropriate, he or she can release monies to or make payments on behalf of the child to cover matters ranging from education, medical and general maintenance.

While court supervision is generally not required with these types of trusts, serving as a trustee can be more onerous than simply serving as a custodian under the UTMA. For example, a trustee is required to file annual income tax returns for the child trust with the IRS. Also, because the powers of trustees of a child's trust are set out in the will or trust document itself, it will be necessary for the trustee to produce copies of the relevant document every time he or she has to deal with a financial institution on behalf the minor child. By contrast, given that the powers of a UTMA custodian are provided for under statute, the majority of banks and other institutions are more familiar with their terms and are more knowledgeable of the authority given to custodians under these statutes.

Children's Pot Trusts

A pot trust is a good tool to use with younger children. Pot trusts are a legal device that allows you to place monies in trust to benefit two or more of your minor children. Pot trusts, however, are somewhat unique in that trust assets are made available to whichever child needs them most rather than being divided equally for the benefit of each child. With a pot trust, your trustee has discretion to apportion the trust funds between the children as he or she sees fit. So, for example, if one of your children wishes to go to college, your trustee can take a portion of the money from the trust to send that child to college. Similarly, should one of your children require an expensive medical treatment, monies can be released from the trust to cover the costs of the treatment.

A pot trust will terminate when the youngest child reaches a specified age (known as the age of termination of the trust) usually, 18 to 30 years of age. At that time, the trust is divided between the children equally.

One of the principal drawbacks to using a pot trust is that older children will not receive their share of the balance of the trust property until the youngest child reaches the designated age of termination of the trust. As such, they may well be into adulthood by the time they receive their shares of the inheritance.

Providing for Children With Special Needs

Surprisingly, less than one in ten parents of special needs children prepare a proper estate plan despite the fact that special needs children will continue to require care well after they reach the age of majority in their states, often for their entire lives. This statistic becomes far more worrying when we consider the strict disability conditions mandated by federal statute. For example, it will come as a surprise to many but if you leave more than $2,000 to a child or adult dependent with special needs, that individual could lose their eligibility for most, if not all, government benefits!

If you are the parent of a special needs child, you can circumvent this situation by including a "special needs trust" in your estate plan. The purpose of this trust is to provide for the disabled child, or adult, without risking that person's eligibility for federal benefits – including that all important healthcare coverage. The trust circumvents the problem by ensuring that the legal title to the trust property is not vested in the eligible child. Rather, since a trust is used, legal title to the trust assets will vest in the trustee. As such, when it comes to assessing the child's entitlement to federal benefits, these assets will not be taken into consideration because they are legally held by the trustee. Meanwhile, the trustee will be authorized under the terms of the special needs trust document to spend money on behalf of and generally to provide for the child. These funds will of course come from the trust fund.

Special needs' planning requires an in-depth knowledge of both the law and benefit entitlements. As such, and while you can do the research yourself, we recommend that you consult with a special needs legal specialist in this area.

Whom Should You Choose as a Trustee?

A trustee's duties can continue for a number of years and, in many cases, may require expertise in investing money, dealing with real estate, paying bills, filing accounts and managing money on behalf of the trusts underlying beneficiaries. As such, you will need to carefully consider your choice of proposed trustee. In many cases, people who establish a trust tend to choose a family member or close friend as they tend not to charge fees for carrying out the role. This is absolutely fine so long as the person is capable of handling the financial matters involved and has sufficient time to carry out the role – and of course is willing to do so…remember to check with them first!

Professional trustees, on the other hand, will charge annual management fees for providing trustee services. In some instances, these fees can be quite substantial. However, given the expertise that a professional trustee can bring to the table, it is important to at least consider engaging them where you have a large estate.

If you decide not to engage a professional trustee and opt for a family member or friend instead, then the characteristics that you should look for in your nominee are honesty, intelligence, diligence and conscientiousness. Having these qualities, above all else, will at least go some way towards ensuring that you pick the right person for the job!

Trustee's Duties

Trustees may have many duties attached to their role. A trustee occupies a fiduciary position (a position of trust) and is therefore bound to act for the benefit of another. Some specific duties include the following:

- **Duty to Adhere to the Terms of the Trust**
  While this may appear to be a very obvious statement, it is surprising how often trustees' decisions are made without referring back to the documents establishing the trust. The trust documents should indicate whether the act in question is permitted under the terms of the trust or not.

- **Duty to Act Personally**
  Unless the trust terms permit, trustees must act personally and may not delegate the performance of tasks or the making of decisions concerning the trust – although the trustee is normally permitted to take professional advice where required.

- **Duty to Act in the Best Interests of the Beneficiaries**
  A trustee is required to act impartially and in the best interests of the trust's beneficiaries. If a trustee fails to do so, he or she could find themselves exposed to a lawsuit instituted by a beneficiary seeking a court review of the trustee's acts and/or omissions. Such a review could result in the trustee losing any compensation which he or she was entitled to receive under the terms of the trust document or even in the trustee being removed from office.

- **Duty to Account**
  Trustees are required to keep full and proper records of the trust –

including all transactions carried out by the trust and all distributions and returns made by it.

- **Duty to Supply Information**

  The beneficiaries of a trust are entitled to certain information regarding the trust. While you may, in your will or living trust document, specify the precise information to which your beneficiaries are entitled, they are usually entitled to a copy of the trust deed, latest financial accounts, copies of title documents relating to trust assets and details of distributions made from the trust to beneficiaries. However, trustees are not normally required to provide explanations for their decisions, minutes of trustee meetings (if any), correspondence between trustees and other beneficiaries or a copy of any memorandum of wishes provided by the creator of the trust.

- **Duty to Invest Prudently**

  In managing the affairs of others, trustees are required to exercise the due care, diligence and skill that a prudent person would ordinarily exercise in the management of other people's assets. This applies equally in the context of investing the trust's assets.

  As a trustee is under a duty to preserve the value of the trust's assets, he or she may need to make appropriate investments to avoid deflation and devaluation of the trust assets. The trustee must exercise due care and diligence in choosing the investments; and where appropriate should obtain professional investment advice.

- **Duty to Carry Out Duties Without Payment**

  Save in respect of out of pocket expenses, trustees are generally required to act without payment unless the trust terms provide otherwise. This is partly why so many people appoint friends and relatives as trustees. Professional trustees, on other hand, will always ensure that the trust documentation contains appropriate powers for the trustee to receive remuneration before they act.

- **Duty to Not Benefit Personally from the Trust**

  As a fiduciary, a trustee may not benefit personally unless the trust document specifically allows for this. This is echoed by the requirement that trustees act in good faith and avoid conflicts of interest which could adversely affect the trustee's decisions. If a conflict of interest does arise, the trustee should always act carefully and, in particular, should consider taking professional advice. In certain instances, the trustee may be able to act where he has made a full disclosure of his interests to all beneficiaries and has obtained their written consent to the transaction in question which gives rise to the conflict.

CHAPTER 3:
GIFTS AND BENEFICIARIES

Chapter Overview

In this chapter, we will share a few thoughts on choosing your beneficiaries as well as look at some of the restrictions that might apply when it comes to making gifts. We will also look at the legal rights of spouses and children and your ability to disinherit them.

CHAPTER 3

GIFTS AND BENEFICIARIES

Gifting Your Assets

Once you've taken the time to make a list of all your assets, the next step in the estate planning process is to consider who you want to gift those assets to. For the most part, you are generally free to gift your assets as you wish. However, there are some restrictions on this freedom. For example, in many states, spouses have a legal entitlement to a certain proportion of their deceased spouse's estate. If you are married, this of course is something that you will need to take into account when preparing your distribution plan.

Further issues arise in the context of children. Under the laws of many states, if you fail to make provision for your children, they may be able to successfully litigate against your estate and obtain an order providing for the redistribution of your assets to include an appropriate share for them. There are ways and means to get around this danger and we'll look at them later in this chapter.

Another thing that you will need to watch out for when making gifts is the age of the beneficiary. As mentioned earlier, most states impose restrictions on minor beneficiaries receiving substantial assets. As such, it becomes necessary to appoint a trustee or guardian who will manage the minor's inheritance until he or she becomes old enough to do so.

As you will have gathered from the foregoing, there are some rules and legalities surrounding the making of gifts. So, to properly prepare your estate plan, you need to have at least a broad understanding of how a gift can be made and what matters might impact the making of that gift. We'll look at these very issues in the ensuing pages.

How to Make a Gift

There are three principal ways in which you can make a gift to someone following your death including under a will, a living trust or under a survivorship designation (e.g. life insurance policies, pay-on-death accounts, joint tenancies, etc). While a survivorship designation is relatively straight forward, the making of gifts under both wills and living trusts is a little more complicated and there are some basic 'gifting rules' which need to be followed. You will also need to have a general understanding of the types of gifts that can be made under a will and living trust as well as the different types of beneficiary under each device. We'll examine each of these in turn below.

Types of Gifts

Simply put, a gift can generally be defined as a voluntary transfer of property from one person to another made gratuitously, without any consideration or compensation. Under your will or living trust, you can leave gifts of either financial or personal value to your family and friends. These gifts can come in the form of gifts of a specific item, gifts of cash or gifts of the residuary of your estate or trust estate.

 Important Note

Your estate is the total sum of your possessions, property and money held in your name (minus debts) at the time of your death. Your trust estate, on the other hand, means all of the assets owned by a trust (such as your living trust) at the time of your death.

The main classifications of gifts are set out below:

Specific Item Gifts

(also known as a demonstrative legacies or specific bequests)

A specific item gift is a gift of a specific item to a named beneficiary. Gifts of this type typically include specific items of personal property you own such as, for example, a car, a piece of jewelry, stocks, bonds, real estate and so on. Needless to say, when drafting your will or living trust, it is important to ensure that you clearly identify and describe the property that you wish to gift. So, for example, where you are gifting a car, you should describe the make, model and color of the car rather than simply referring to "my car". This reduces the risk of confusion over what you intended – especially if you have more than one car at the time of your death! When writing a provision for a gift, a good question to ask yourself is whether a stranger reading your will or living trust would easily understand exactly what you wanted to gift. If not, you need to re-write that clause!

Cash Gifts

(also known as monetary or pecuniary legacies)

A cash gift is a gift of a specific amount of money or cash to a named beneficiary. Just as with specific items gifts, when making a cash gift you need to clearly specify the amount that you are gifting (including the currency) and the person to whom you wish to make the gift to. In addition, when making a cash gift, it is important that you consider the financial implications on the overall estate. Remember, you may need to ensure that sufficient funds are readily available to meet the needs of your dependents or to discharge any taxes or expenses (including funeral expenses) which might be payable following your death. So be careful not to exhaust your cash too quickly – otherwise other assets may need to be sold to raise funds to discharge these obligations.

Gift of the Residuary Estate

This is simply a gift of the residue of an estate or trust estate to one or more named beneficiaries. The residue of an estate (or residuary estate, as it is often called) is the remainder of a deceased person's estate after the payment of all debts, funeral and testamentary expenses and after all specific item and cash gifts have been made. The residue of your trust estate is exactly the same except that it's the balance of your trust estate after all gifts and payments have been made from your trust.

 Warning

> The residue of an estate or trust estate is that part of the estate or trust estate which remains after the payment of all debts and expenses, and after making the transfer of all specific gifts and cash gifts.

A residuary also includes property that is the subject of a failed gift. A gift fails in circumstances where the beneficiary has died or refuses their right to the gift. The person entitled to receive a gift of the residuary estate under a will or residuary trust estate under a living trust is called the residuary beneficiary or, if there is more than one beneficiary, residuary beneficiaries.

Types of Beneficiaries

A beneficiary is a person, organization or other entity that will inherit part of your assets or estate under your will or living trust.

There are three principal types of beneficiaries under a will or living trust. These include a specific gift beneficiary, an alternate beneficiary and a residuary beneficiary.

Specific Gift Beneficiary

A specific gift beneficiary is a person or organization named in your will or living trust to receive a specific item gift or a specific cash gift as defined above. Specific gifts are generally the first gifts distributed under a will or living trust. Any assets that are not specifically distributed under your will or living trust form part of the residue (assuming that you have a catch all residuary clause – see below) and will usually be given (unless there are taxes or other expenses to be discharged) to the person or persons named as residuary beneficiaries in each case.

Alternate Beneficiary

When naming beneficiaries to receive gifts under your will or living trust, it's prudent (but not obligatory) to prepare for the possibility that one or more of these beneficiaries will be unable (whether due to death or otherwise) or unwilling (for whatever reason) to accept the gifts made to them. To this end, it is helpful to nominate alternate beneficiaries to receive the gift in the event that the primary beneficiary is unable or unwilling to do so. An alternate beneficiary is a person who becomes legally entitled to inherit a gift if the first named beneficiary is unable or unwilling to accept the gift. Alternate beneficiaries are the second class of beneficiaries to inherit under your will or living trust.

A beneficiary who refuses to accept a gift is said to have 'disclaimed' their entitlement to a gift. It is advisable to have all such disclaimers in writing before the gift is passed to the alternate beneficiary.

Here are a few examples of situations where it might make sense to name alternate beneficiaries:

- you've left something to someone who has a dangerous occupation and there is a risk that this person might predecease you;

- you have left something substantial or meaningful to somebody older than you who is likely to predecease you; or

- you left a gift to someone with an illness that may or may not claim their lives.

You are entirely free to name more than one person as an alternate beneficiary. You can even appoint a second alternate to receive a gift where the first alternate is unable or unwilling to accept it. However, when doing this it is important that you fully consider the order in which the alternate beneficiaries become entitled to share the property and ensure that this order is correct.

Residuary Beneficiary

A residuary beneficiary is the person(s) or organization(s) named to receive the residue of your estate or trust estate; they get what's left when all of the specific gifts have been made and all debts and taxes paid.

Who May Not Be a Beneficiary?

While you are generally free to make gifts to anyone you choose, the law does place some restrictions on the people who can receive gifts from you under your will. In particular, the following persons or organizations will be precluded from receiving gifts from you under your will:

- a lawyer who is involved in drafting your will or in providing counsel to you in connection with your will. If such a lawyer was permitted to receive a gift under the terms of your will, the presumption would be raised, as a matter of law, that your lawyer exerted some form of undue influence over you which caused you to name him or her as a beneficiary under your will. To prevent such abuses of influence, lawyers involved in the preparation of your will, as aforesaid, are prohibited from inheriting under it. If you have a lawyer relative or friend that you wish to benefit under your will, it is advisable that you hire a third-party attorney to draft your will for you; and that you simply don't consult with or engage your lawyer relative or friend in relation to the matter.

    The prohibition on making gifts to your lawyer friend or relative does not apply to the appointment of executors. You can still appoint this person as an executor of your estate and direct that he or she is paid for carrying out their duties as executor;

- any person who has witnessed the signing of your will. This prohibition also extends to include the spouses of any such witnesses.

The prohibition has its origins in old English rules of evidence, upon which U.S. common law is partly based. These rules provided that parties nominated as beneficiaries under a will could not testify in court as to the proper execution of that will due to their conflict of interest. This is because there was a fear that their testimony could be influenced by the value of the gifts that the testator left to them under the will. Obviously, if they stood to inherit a windfall, the witnesses were more likely to testify that all the formalities associated with signing the will were strictly complied with and that, as a result, the will was valid. Of course, the opposite scenario is also likely!

As a result of these rules, gifts to witnesses or their spouses under a will are rendered null and void in the majority of states. As such, it is recommended that none of the witnesses to your will or their spouses, or even relatives, should stand to benefit under your will as they will most likely be prohibited from receiving the gift made to them. If you wish to leave them a gift, it's recommended that you either use alternative witnesses or that you leave the gift to them under the terms of a codicil and that alternate persons witness your execution of that codicil;

 Did You Know?

A codicil is a document that amends, rather than replaces, a previously executed will. The formalities associated with executing a codicil are almost identical to that associated with executing a will.

- any person who unlawfully caused your death; and

- an unincorporated association that is not permitted to hold property. This is important to note in the context of making gifts to clubs and other unincorporated organizations. Before you make such gifts to such organizations, you should check with the secretary of that organization to ensure it has sufficient powers to receive the gift.

Changing Beneficiaries

Unless required by law, you have no legal duty to leave your property to anyone. It follows therefore that you are more or less free to change the beneficiaries of your estate or trust estate whenever you like to whomever you like. Of course, there are some exceptions when it comes to spouses and children. Generally though, most people find that they do not need or wish to make many, if any, changes.

Yet changes are sometimes required. For example, if one or more of your beneficiaries die, or you dispose of a specific item of property (that you had left to a particular beneficiary), or if you neglected to nominate alternate beneficiaries, you wish to amend your will or living trust to add new beneficiaries or alternate beneficiaries, or even to make new gifts. Amending your documents is relatively straightforward.

To amend a will, you can either make a new will in its entirety or you can make a codicil which will amend a specific portion of your existing will. A codicil simply records the changes you wish to make to your will; and is executed in the same way as a will. Living trusts on the other hand can be amended by an amendment agreement (if the trust is created under an agreement) or a deed of amendment (if the trust is created under a deed). Again, similar to a codicil, the agreement or deed simply records the changes to be made to the original document.

Gifts to Spouses

Before making a gift to your spouse, or indeed to any one, it is important to understand the rights which surviving spouses have over their deceased spouse's estate; as well as the basic differences in distribution of property in both common law and community property states. We'll look at these matters below.

Community Property States

Property owned by couples in community property states is divided loosely into two categories - separate property and community property.

A spouse's separate property is all property acquired by that spouse before or after he or she got married (including after a legal separation) plus all property received as a gift or an inheritance and maintained separately (i.e. not jointly with his or her spouse) during that marriage. Community property, on the other hand, is all other property earned or acquired by either spouse during the marriage.

Important Note

At the date of writing there are nine community property states namely Arizona, California, Idaho, Louisiana, Nevada, New Mexico, Texas, Washington and Wisconsin. In Alaska couples can opt to have their property treated as community property under the terms of a written property agreement. The property distribution rules in these states may also apply to registered domestic partners.

Separate property can also be deemed community property where it is formerly transferred by one spouse to the joint names of both spouses. Similarly, where property is gifted to one spouse and subsequently commingled with community property, the property can become community property.

Each of Alaska, Arizona, California, Nevada, Texas and Wisconsin allow a surviving spouse or domestic partner to automatically inherit community property when the other spouse or partner dies provided that property's title document makes it clear that the property is owned as community property with a right of survivorship in favor of the surviving spouse.

Normally, classifying property as community or separate property is relatively straightforward. However there are a number of instances in which the classification is not clear. These include the ownership of businesses, companies, pensions, the proceeds of certain lawsuits, and incomes received from separate property. In cases such as these, you should consult a local attorney to determine how your state treats these items.

The majority of community property states do not grant a surviving spouse a legal right to inherit from the deceased spouse's estate. Rather, what they do is try to divide the marital assets (or registered partnership assets) during the lifetime of the spouses (or partners) by classifying certain assets as community property. Each spouse (or partner) in turn is deemed to own 50% of the community property.

However, in each of Alaska, California, Idaho, Washington and Wisconsin a surviving spouse or domestic partner may elect to receive a specific portion of the deceased spouse's community or separate property in limited circumstances. For more information on such entitlements, we recommend that you consult a lawyer.

Warning

If you are in a registered domestic partnership and considering a move to another state, you should pay close attention to the laws of the state into which you are proposing to move as the 'new state' may not recognize the property rights which you had in your 'old state'. If you are in any doubt as to how the law will affect you, you should consult a practicing lawyer in your area.

Common Law States

In common law states, each spouse owns all property acquired using their own income and all property legally registered solely in their name. Any property, such as your marital home for example, registered in the names of both spouses is deemed owned jointly. If you reside in a common law state, your spouse has a legal right to a fraction of your estate upon your passing. Depending on which state you reside in, this legal right will usually amount to between one-third and one-half of your estate. The precise amount to which your spouse is entitled will also depend on whether you have any minor children and whether your spouse has been provided for outside the terms of your will or living trust.

The legal right of your spouse will take priority over any devises or legacies made in your will or your living trust, and will rank in priority after creditors of your estate. Your spouse will be entitled to either exercise his or her legal right to receive the specified fraction of your estate which he or she is entitled to or waive that right in favor of whatever has been left to him or her under the terms of your will and/or living trust.

The right of your spouse to take a defined percentage of your estate does not arise by the operation of law; rather it must be proactively elected. This means that your spouse must 'speak up' and state that he or she wishes to exercise this right rather than accept what has been left to them under the terms of your will or living trust. Of course, any such election should be in writing and signed by your spouse. If your spouse fails to elect to take his or her legal share within the time frames set out under law, then he or she will be obliged to accept the gifts you have left to him or her under your will and/or living trust. Separately, your spouse can also waive his or her rights to this entitlement if he or she wishes.

Matters in relation to elections of a legal right can become more complex when a couple moves from a common law state to a community property state. In California, Idaho, Washington and Wisconsin, property acquired prior to a move will be treated as if it had been acquired in the state to which you have moved. In other community property states, the property will be treated in accordance with the laws of the state in which it was acquired. As you no doubt have gathered, this can result in marital property being subjected to both common law and community property rules. In such cases, it is important that care is taken to determine which laws affect what types of property before you commence making your will or transferring property to your living trust.

By contrast, couples that move from a community property state to a common law state come up against the opposite problem. In such cases, each spouse retains a 50% interest in the community property acquired while the couple was resident in the community property state.

In addition to a surviving spouse's entitlement to claim a defined portion of their deceased spouse's estate, they also have a number of additional entitlements which we will discuss later in this chapter.

Gifts to Minors

Depending on your state's laws, minor children may only receive a nominal amount of property in their own names under the terms of a will, living trust or otherwise on a person's death. The amount varies from state to state but is usually between $1,000 and $5,000. If you leave a gift to a minor in excess of the permitted statutory amount, it will be necessary either by the terms of your will, trust or by a court order, to appoint a custodian, trustee or property guardian to manage those assets on behalf of the minor child. For more information on property management for minors, refer to Chapter 2.

Unmarried or Same-Sex Couples

Save in a few states, unmarried couples or same sex couples usually don't have any legal right to inherit their partner's property – no matter how long they have been together. As such, it's important for people in these types of relationship to arrange their estate planning so that property is left to their partner. This can be done using a will, a living trust or through a beneficiary designation on a bank account, investment account or insurance policy. Of course, they could also re-register property in their joint names and add a survivorship designation to the title documents.

Gifts to Charities

We all know of numerous charities that raise proceeds for a variety of good causes. In raising these proceeds, charities rely on the generosity of corporate sponsors and members of the public. Without this funding, many charities would simply not be able to carry on the valuable work they are doing. So, while you will naturally want to make appropriate provision for your family and friends in your estate planning documents, you may also want to make a gift (or at least consider doing so) to your favorite charity as well. This can be easily done under your will or living trust.

Making a gift is simple. All you do is identify the gift you wish to make and the charity that will receive the gift. You can gift money, specific items or nominate the charity as a beneficiary of the residuary of your estate or trust estate – the choice is yours!

However, where you choose to make a gift to a charity it's important to ensure that you provide clear details of the charity to be benefited. In this respect, it is useful to identity the charity by reference to its correct legal name (as it may differ from the 'trading name' commonly used by the charity) as well as its charity registration number.

It is worth mentioning that a number of states impose limitations on leaving large portions of your estate to charity. Therefore it is advisable to consult a lawyer if you wish to leave 50% or more of your estate to a charitable institution or a not-for-profit organization.

Failed Gifts

If you decide to gift a specific item to a beneficiary and you or the trust (as the case may be) subsequently dispose of the item before your death then, upon your death, the gift will fail because it cannot be completed. Where the gift fails, the intended beneficiary will not be entitled to receive a substitute gift unless you have expressly provided for this in your will or living trust. Additionally, if you gift a specific item or a particular amount of money to a named person and that person predeceases you then, unless an alternate beneficiary is entitled to receive that gift under the terms of your will or living trust, the gift reverts to form part of your residuary estate or residuary trust estate, as the case may be.

Imposing Conditions on the Receipt of Gifts

In making a gift under your will or living trust, you may wish to provide that the beneficiary will only be entitled to receive that gift if certain conditions are satisfied. While this is perfectly acceptable, it can be somewhat difficult to police.

There are two basic types of conditions that can be imposed on a beneficiary - conditions precedent and conditions subsequent.

A condition precedent is a requirement that must be met before the beneficiary is entitled to receive a gift. For example, you may specify that, "*I give the sum of $5,000 to my nephew John Doe if he has obtained a college degree in engineering before 31 December 2020. If my nephew John Doe has not obtained the college degree as aforesaid, then I give the sum of $5,000 to my niece Jane Doe instead*". The imposition of such a condition does not pose to many difficulties for the executor or trustee as it will be easy to determine whether the beneficiary has met the requirement or not…. of course they may have to wait a while to find out. If the beneficiary fails to meet the requirements, then the proceeds being held by the executor or trustee to make this gift will be given to the persons entitled to the residuary interest in the estate or trust estate.

A condition subsequent, on the other hand, is a requirement that must be met after the beneficiary receives the gift. These types of conditions cause a lot more problems than conditions precedent because often the gift is received on the condition that the beneficiary fulfils an obligation or a specific event occurs. Of course, problems arise where the obligation is not fulfilled or the event never occurs.

If we took our example above and modified the condition such that it became a condition subsequent, it would read something like this "*I give the sum of $5,000 to my nephew John Doe on the conditions that he uses this money to obtain a college degree in engineering before 31 December 2020. If my nephew John Doe has not obtained the college degree as aforesaid, then I give the sum of $5,000 to my niece Jane Doe instead*". In this instance, John has received the gift before he has satisfied the condition. This of course can be problematic. What happens if John fails to satisfy the condition within the required time frame? Well, Jane Doe will need to try and recover the $5,000 from John. This may be easier said than done of course.

While most conditions placed on the receipt of a gift are generally valid, there are some conditions that courts will refuse to enforce. Typically, these are conditions that are void for uncertainty (i.e. they are unclear) or void on the grounds of public policy. Conditions void on the grounds of public policy would, for example, include requirements that the beneficiary marry or refrain from marrying someone, divorce or refrain from divorcing someone, change religion or even murder someone.

A common restriction placed on beneficiaries comes in the form of a no-contest clause in a will or living trust. Under a no-contest clause any beneficiary who challenges your will or living trust can lose all his or her right to inherit under that instrument. Without this clause, if a beneficiary is unhappy with their gift, they can sue the estate or trust estate and still be entitled to receive their original gift afterwards even where they lose – but, by that time, the estate will have decreased in value because it has had to incur legal fees and costs in defending the action.

Disinheritance

While the laws vary lightly from state to state, it's generally only a spouse that has any real entitlement to inherit from a deceased person's estate after they die. Surprisingly for some, children do not automatically have a right to inherit from their parents.

For one reason or another, many people consider disinheriting family members – often because of some underlying dispute. It's therefore important to look at how the laws work in this area so that you can, if you so wish, disinherit family members to the fullest extent permitted by law. We'll do just that in the ensuing pages.

Disinheriting a Spouse

As discussed above, the laws of most states allow a surviving spouse the choice of choosing between what he or she has been left under the terms of his or her deceased spouse's will or receiving a specific share of the deceased spouse's estate as defined by statute. This share is known as the minimum or "elective" share. While the amount of this share tends to vary from state to state, the general rule is that if a deceased spouse had no children the surviving would be entitled to half of the deceased spouse's net estate. On the other hand, where the deceased spouse had children, the surviving spouse would have an entitlement to claim one third of the deceased spouse's net estate. Some states also impose financial thresholds. For example, under New York law, a surviving souse is entitled to $50,000 or one third of the deceased spouse's net estate, whichever is the greater.

Did You Know?

Divorce terminates the right of election by the surviving spouse.

Where the deceased spouse leaves more than the elective share of the net estate to the surviving spouse, he or she will generally not exercise the right of election unless he or she believed that it would be more advantageous to allow a greater part of the deceased spouse's estate to pass to the other beneficiaries named in the will, for tax reasons or otherwise. Of course, the surviving spouse's right of election is really only valuable where the deceased spouse left less than the elective share to the surviving spouse. Consider, for example, the situation where a husband dies leaving everything to his children and nothing his spouse. In such a case, the surviving spouse would under New York law, for example, have the right to receive the elective share (i.e., the greater of $50,000 or one-third of the estate) notwithstanding the terms of the deceased spouse's will or living trust. The consequence of this is that the amount of the deceased spouse's estate passing to the children would be reduced. It may even be the case that certain beneficiaries no longer receive a gift from the deceased spouse!

If a surviving spouse elects to take his or her legal share rather than take what was left to him or her under the terms of the deceased spouse's will, then he or she generally forfeits the right to receive anything under the will. However, in many cases where an election is made, the surviving spouse will often be allowed take some or all of the items (depending on what was gifted to the surviving spouse) left to him or her under the will, particularly in circumstances where the amount left under the will is in fact less than the spouse's elective share. The balance of any amount owing to the surviving spouse is often then made up in cash. Alternatively, he or she can take assets from the residuary estate and so on until the legal share is satisfied. On the other hand, if the spouse elects to take his or her inheritance under the deceased spouse's will he or she will generally be entitled to receive those assets from the estate.

Whichever choice a surviving spouse makes, it's important to remember that they will (unless the terms of the will provides otherwise) still be entitled to avail of their other legal rights which, depending on the state law, include the right to buy certain estate assets, to remain in the principal residence for a specific period of time (usually a year), to claim and receive an allowance for their support, to receive automobiles and watercraft owned by the deceased, and to avail of such other rights as a surviving spouse would ordinarily be entitled to under law.

While in most cases, the election of the surviving spouse will not affect certain non-probate property, such as jointly owned property and property with rights of survivorship attached, pay-on-death accounts and transfer-on-death securities, it may well have an effect on other types of non-probate property such as property held in a trust. That said, in states which have adopted the Uniform Probate Code, certain assets that have passed to the surviving spouse either during the life of the deceased spouse or on the death of the deceased spouse (thorough joint tenancy or on survivorship) are deemed part of the surviving spouse's elective share. You will need to check the laws of the deceased spouse's state of residence to determine what property is included in the surviving spouse's right to elect.

 Did You Know?

The Uniform Probate Code (the "Code") is a statute that unifies the laws governing the transfer of a person's estate. It deals with matters such as probate, transfers on intestacy, transfer of assets outside of probate, legal entitlements of spouses and trust administration. The Code was originally approved by the National Conference of Commissioners on Uniform State Laws and the House of Delegates of the American Bar Association in 1969. Its purpose was to modernize probate law and administration and to encourage uniformity in all fifty states. At the time of this writing, the UPC has been adopted by 18 states in full and by numerous states in part.

Uniform Probate Code - Full State Adoptions		
Alaska	Michigan	North Dakota
Arizona	Minnesota	Pennsylvania
Colorado	Montana	South Carolina
Hawaii	Nebraska	South Dakota
Idaho	New Jersey	Utah
Maine	New Mexico	Wisconsin

As you will have gathered from the foregoing, in most states, the deceased cannot simply disinherit a spouse.

Disinheriting a Child

Much unlike other common law countries, it is however possible to completely disinherit children in virtually every state in the U.S. Only in Louisiana is this restricted. In order to do so, your will (as opposed to your living trust) must either (i) expressly state that you intend to disinherit your child or (ii) make only a nominal gift to your child (such as a gift of $10). If you fail to adopt either of these two approaches and simply don't mention your child in your will at all then you run the risk of your child challenging your will and a court subsequently making a determination that there has been an accidental disinheritance on your part. This could result in a re-distribution of your estate with a large portion potentially going to your child.

If you wish to disinherit your child, it's best to include provisions similar to those mentioned in the preceding paragraph in both your will and your living trust, even where you have transferred all of your assets to your living trust.

Moreover, in some states, the above laws apply not only to your children but also to your grandchildren. This in essence allows grandchildren to challenge the will of a grandparent who failed to provide for them or their dead parent. As such, if your intention is to disinherit your grandchildren, it is important to ensure that the grandchildren are expressly disinherited in the same way as children. Again, mention the disinheritance in both your will and living trust.

In certain circumstances children are entitled to claim a share of a deceased parent's property, regardless of the terms of the parent's will or living trust. For example, if you live in the state of Florida and are the head of your family for tax purposes, you will be prohibited from leaving your home to anyone besides your spouse or children.

Matters Affecting the Distribution of Your Assets

Before you make any decisions on how you wish to distribute your assets, it's useful to be aware of a number of specific events that can have an impact on how your assets are ultimately distributed. These events include the following: -

- simultaneous death;

- homestead allowance;

- family allowance for support;

- the exemption for the benefit of the family;

- right to remain in the family home;

- right to receive family residence;

- right to automobiles;

- right to reimbursement of funeral bill;

- abatement of assets; and

- disclaimed inheritances.

We'll consider each of these further below.

Simultaneous Death

It is common in wills and trusts to insert what is known as 'common disaster' or 'simultaneous death' provisions. These types of provisions usually provide that in order for your beneficiary to receive a gift under your will or trust, they must survive you for a specific period of time, usually 30 to 60 days, before they can inherit from you. These types of clauses are aimed at the situations where, for example, you might die in an accident in which one or more of your named beneficiaries are also mortally injured. If that beneficiary survives you, and there is no required survival period, he or she could be entitled to receive the gift immediately on your death and, in doing so, would be obliged to pay certain estate taxes – which could become owing at the time of your death. If that beneficiary were to die shortly after you, the beneficiary's heirs would in turn be entitled to receive the asset and may well be obliged to pay estate tax on the item - for a second time in quick succession. The provisions are designed to avoid these types of multiple administrations and the payment of estate taxes on the same assets where one of your beneficiaries dies of injuries a few hours (or days) after you.

This common disaster provision is most commonly used between spouses and provides for the transfer of the deceased's estate to the surviving spouse only if the surviving spouse survives the deceased spouse for a certain period of time following the deceased spouse's death. If the surviving spouse does not survive the deceased spouse for the requisite time frame, the assets will most usually pass to children or to other named beneficiaries under the will.

Homestead Allowance

In all states, a surviving spouse is entitled to a cash allowance from the deceased spouse's estate known as a homestead allowance. The amount of the allowance varies from state to state. In some states, the amount is fixed while in other it is dependent on the value of the deceased spouse's estate.

The states which have adopted the Uniform Probate Code typically allow for an allowance of $15,000 as this is what is recommended under the Code. However, as the Code gives discretion to each adopting state to determine the precise amount of the allowance, it does vary from state to state.

Under the Code, if your spouse predeceases you, each of your minor and dependent children is entitled to a pro-rata share of the homestead allowance (the relevant statutory amount, divided by the number of your minor and dependent children).

The homestead allowance is in addition to any share of your estate passing to your surviving spouse or minor or dependent children under your will (unless otherwise provided in your will), by intestate succession, or by way of elective share. It is also exempt from and has priority over all claims against your estate.

Family Allowance for Support

While the law varies from state to state, surviving spouses and dependent children are generally entitled to a cash allowance from a deceased spouse's estate for their maintenance during the period of probate administration. Under the Code, for example, they are entitled to a reasonable amount having regard to their previous standard of living and any other financial resources available to them. In other states, the amount tends to be a fixed monitory sum, such as in Ohio where the amount is $40,000. The allowance itself may be paid as a lump sum or in periodic installments throughout the probate process.

You will need to check the laws of your state to determine the precise level of allowance available to your family.

The Exemption for the Benefit of the Family

In addition to the above rights, a surviving spouse is entitled in certain states to certain property from the deceased spouse's estate (subject to certain monitory limitations) irrespective of whether the deceased spouse's will gives that property to them or not.

For example, in the states that have adopted the Code, the property to which a surviving spouse is entitled includes household furniture, automobiles, furnishings, appliances and personal effects not exceeding $10,000 in value. If any of the property selected is encumbered (i.e. has a debt secured against it) and the value in excess of security interests, plus that of other exempt property, is less than $10,000, or if there is not $10,000 worth of exempt property in the estate, the spouse or children are entitled to other assets of the estate, if any, to the extent necessary to make up the $10,000 threshold.

If there is no surviving spouse, the deceased's children are entitled jointly to the same $10,000 benefit.

Right to Remain in the Family Home

A surviving spouse generally has the right to remain in the family home, if it is a probate asset, for a period of up to one year from the date of death of the deceased spouse. In some states, this period is extended to a right to remain in the family home for life. This applies notwithstanding that the house may have been gifted to someone else under the terms of the deceased spouse's will. However, if it happens that the family home is sold during the administration process to pay debts of the estate, the surviving spouse may be entitled to receive an amount from the estate equal to the fair rental value of the property as compensation for the loss of the right of residence.

The election of the right to remain in the family home must be made by the surviving spouse within a specific time frame following the initial appointment of an executor or else the right lapses. You should check the laws applicable in your state to determine the precise time frames in this respect.

Right to Receive Family Residence

In certain states, depending upon the value of the property, a surviving spouse may have the right to obtain the family residence as part of their inheritance. Moreover, a spouse may also have the right to purchase certain assets of the probate estate at the appraised values.

Right to Automobiles

In a few states, the surviving spouse and/or children of a deceased person may be entitled to receive automobiles from the deceased's estate notwithstanding that they were not left to them under the terms of the deceased's will. In some cases, these assets fall under the entitlement referred to above as being 'for the benefit of the family'. Again, where applicable, this right needs to be exercised within the specific time frames set out under state law.

Right to Reimbursement of Funeral Costs

In some states, a spouse may be entitled to reimbursement by the deceased spouse's estate for the payment of the deceased's funeral costs.

Abatement of Assets

When the residuary of an estate is insufficient to pay the debts and taxes owing by an estate, it will become necessary to apply other assets of the estate to meet these payments. The process by which these assets are applied to pay the debts of the estate is known as abatement. Generally, the first assets of an estate which are abated are legacies (i.e. the cash gifts). For example, if the estate has $50,000 in the bank account to cover cash gifts to the deceased's friends, and debts are still owing by the estate after the residuary estate has been dissipated, the money may be used to discharge these debts. Any of the $50,000 remaining after payment of the debts will be distributed pro rata to the aforementioned beneficiaries. However, if the funds are insufficient to pay off all of the debts, then the executor can begin to sell the items left as specific item gifts (i.e. antiques, jewelry, real estate, etc). There are specific orders in which the gifts can be sold and you will need to check the order which applies in your state for further clarification.

As you will have gathered, the net result following the abatement process is that people who have been left gifts under your will may not receive anything if the estate has high levels of debt. As such, in formulating your estate plan, you need to carefully consider the debt levels of your estate and even designate which assets you would like sold to meet those debts if there are insufficient reserves in the residuary estate to meet the payments.

Disclaimed Inheritances

A beneficiary can renounce or disclaim their entitlement to receive a gift under a will or trust. This may be done for several reasons - because it's unwanted, carries heavy liabilities (property maintenance, for example), tax reasons, or because the intended beneficiary simply wants to pass the gift to another beneficiary. If an alternate beneficiary has been named in your will or trust to receive that gift, he or she will then become entitled to it. If no alternate beneficiary is named, the gift will be passed to the beneficiary or beneficiaries entitled to the residue of the estate.

Finalizing Your Plan

Before finalizing your estate plan, it is important to talk with your family. One good reason for this is that it can often help resolve many potential disputes and worries before they arise. The perspective of a spouse or respected family member or friend, who knows you well, may help you reach decisions that you would not have reached on your own. Often, two (or more) heads are better than one.

Also, as difficult as it can be at the time, it is better to clear the air, and bring things out in the open. If you express your intentions regarding your property and sentimental distributions you prepare your beneficiaries and those who will not be beneficiaries, for what to expect following your death.

The occurrence of family discussions is also useful in detecting and later planning to defend or divert possible challenges to your will or living trust. After you have discussed your estate plan and assessed your family's reaction to it, it will be imperative to ask yourself, *"is there any realistic likelihood of anyone challenging my will or living trust?"*

Ordinarily you should have nothing to worry about but there are particular scenarios of which you should be aware and of which you should keep in mind.

Lawsuits By Spouses

If you do not leave your spouse an appropriate amount of your property, having regard to the specific requirements to do so under state law, he or she may have a legal right to bring a lawsuit against your estate or trust estate to claim their lawful inheritance. This will no doubt be one of the most difficult things to discuss with others but there are certain people in your family or friendship circles that it may very well pay you to discuss this matter with.

Disinheriting Your Children

As with Dame Roddick, some people do not wish to leave much (or indeed anything) to a particular child or children. Technically children have no right to inherit anything from their parents, but there are exceptions and a surprised and disgruntled child may try to find those exceptions. More often, a disinherited child may feel they have been unintentionally overlooked and seek to "remedy the mistake".

It is felt by many that the best way to handle such a sensitive matter is to leave some small amount to the child rather than nothing at all. Others recommend that the parents document the reasons for disinheriting their child in their will. If a small amount of money is left, you may insert a no-contest clause and state your reasons for the minimal bequest. If this is the path you feel you should follow it is strongly suggested that you seek professional legal help.

There are those who do not wish to leave their children anything, some for very justifiable reasons. Your intentions should be discussed with other family members, who may be able to give you some very helpful feedback regarding your intentions.

CHAPTER 4:
LAST WILL AND TESTAMENT

Chapter Overview

In this chapter, you will learn about the different types of wills and the main issues that you will need to consider when making a will. We also look at the legal consequences of dying without a will.

Chapter 4

CHAPTER 4

LAST WILL AND TESTAMENT

About Wills

A will, more formally known as a last will and testament, is a legal document that expresses your desires and intentions regarding the distribution of your real and personal property following your death. Real property is generally immovable property such as real estate, homes, land and land improvements. Personal property, on the other hand, includes your movable property such as stocks, bonds, jewelry, furniture, clothing, artwork, etc. Basically, it is your will that determines how, when and even why you want this property apportioned between your relatives, friends and charities. In most cases, your heirs must honor the instructions set out in your will regarding the distribution of your property.

 Did You Know?

Historically, a 'will' document was used to transfer real property following a person's death, while a 'testament' document was used only in relation to the disposition of personal property. However, the two documents merged over time to become a single document known as a 'last will and testament'.

In addition to the distribution of your property, your will also appoints one or more people to act as your executor. Your executor will be charged with the task of carrying out the instructions set out in your will and winding up your affairs generally following your death.

Without a will, the decisions as to how your estate will be distributed and who will act as executor will be made by a court in accordance with your state's intestacy laws (i.e. the laws that apply where a person dies without a valid will).

As author of your will you are known as the 'testator' as you are "attesting" to your wishes as set out in your will. The term 'testator' has become gender neutral over the years and as such it refers to both male and female will makers. That said, it is not uncommon to see the female designation of the word ('testatrix') used, particularly in older wills.

Principal Components of a Will

Standard wills are normally comprised of a number of essential components. These essential components are supplemented and personalized by a number of ancillary clauses that are specific to your own particular circumstances.

Standard wills typically contain the following clauses:

- **Preamble*** - sets out the name and addresses of the testator;

- **Revocation*** – revokes all previous wills and other testamentary documents made by the testator;

- **Executor*** - appoints a person (or persons) known as an executor(s) (or a personal representative) to wind up the testator's affairs following his or her death;

- **Survivorship** – a common clause that requires beneficiaries under a will to survive the testator by a fixed period of time, such as 30 days, before they become entitled to inherit under the testator's will. This clause is commonly used in connection with gifts made by one spouse to the other and serves as a means of reducing multiple estate administrations and the possible double payment of estate taxes in respect of the same assets;

- **Cash gift (legacy***)* – makes a gift of cash;

- **Specific property gift (bequest)** – makes a gift of a specific item of property;

- **Residue*** – makes a gift of all assets passing through the residuary estate to one or more beneficiaries;

- **Estate administration and expenses** – specifies the means by which the testator's estate is to pay the debts, expenses, taxes and costs of estate administration;

- **UTMA and Child trusts** – create a type of trust to manage property gifted to minor beneficiaries under the terms of the testator's will;

- **Guardianship** – appoints guardians and successor guardians to care for the testator's minor children;

- **Executive powers*** – sets out the powers to be granted to the executor(s);

- **Executors' fees** – specifies whether the executor(s) should be compensated for their work, or held liable in the event of incurring a loss of estate funds;

- **Attestation*** – the place where the testator signs and executes the will; and

- **Witnessing*** – the place where the witnesses (usually two) sign and attest that they have witnessed the testator sign the will.

* = these items should appear in every will!

Types of Wills

There are numerous different types of wills currently in use today. Some wills, such as simple wills and testamentary trust wills, are recognized as legal in all states, while others are not. You will need to check with your attorney or check your state laws to see which types of will are valid in your state.

The principal types of wills in use today include the following:

Simple Wills

This is the most common type of will made in the United States and, as the name implies, usually only provides for the distribution of an estate, the appointment of an executor and, if required, the appointment of guardians for minor children.

Testamentary Trust Wills

This is a will that provides for the establishment of a trust upon the death of the testator. On the testator's death, certain or all of his or her assets will be transferred into a trust which will thereafter be administered by trustees appointed under the will in accordance with the terms of the will. This type of will is often used to provide for a spouse or young children.

Pour-Over Wills

A pour-over will is most commonly used with trusts, such as living trusts. It is designed to transfer some or all of the testator's assets to a trust fund following his or her death. The trust fund, in turn, will provide for the management and/or distribution of those assets. Unlike testamentary trust wills, these trusts are not created upon the testator's death, nor are their terms contained within the will document itself. Rather, these trusts are created before the testator dies under a separate trust deed or agreement. The most common example of a trust of this type is a living trust.

Self-Proving Wills

In the normal course, a will is presented to the Probate Court as part of the probate process. If there is any doubt as to the authenticity of the signature of the testator appearing on a will, the court may call upon the persons who witnessed the execution of the will to certify in court that the signature of the testator appearing on the will is in fact authentic and that the will was validly executed. One way of avoiding having to call these witnesses to court is to pre-validate the testator's signature. To do this, both the testator and the witnesses sign a document called an 'affidavit'. This is little more than a document in which the witnesses acknowledge that they witnessed the testator sign the will. However, the big difference is that it is signed in the presence of a notary who, in turn, officially seals the document to give it authenticity. The court will normally accept the execution of a will with an accompanying affidavit as genuine. The affidavit, when attached to the related will, is generally called a 'self-proving will'.

Holographic Wills

Holographic wills are wills that have been written in the testator's own hand writing. However, unlike most other wills, they do not need to be witnessed. This type of will is not valid in every state and, even where they are valid, we generally recommend that you avoid using them unless absolutely necessary in the circumstances.

Oral Wills

As the name suggests, this is a will that is verbally spoken rather than written down on paper. Very few states recognize the validity of such wills and, of those that do, most only recognize an oral will to be valid where it is made during a final illness and in respect of personal property that has a relatively low monetary value.

Joint Wills

A joint or mutual will is a single document incorporating the instructions of any two people, usually spouses, in relation to the disposal of both of their estates. The big problem with joint wills is that once one of the testators die, the terms of the will cannot be changed. This means that the surviving testator is locked into the distribution provisions set out in the will in relation to the assets covered by the will. He or she cannot change the will even where their circumstances have changed and same is warranted. We do not recommend the use of joint wills and suggest the use of two separate wills in its place.

Mirror Wills

A mirror will is a will that essentially mirrors the provisions of another will. These types of wills are most commonly used by a husband and wife who wish to make almost identical provisions in relation to the distribution of their estates. For example, they may well wish to leave everything to the other if they die or, if both of them die together, to named beneficiaries (usually children). Unlike joint wills, each spouse or partner is free to change their will at any time, even following the death of the other spouse or partner.

Living Wills

Despite its name, this really isn't a will in the normal sense. For example, unlike normal wills, which come into effect or speak from the date of death of the author, a living will applies while the author is still alive. Even more different is its function. While normal wills tend to dispose of property, the effect of a living will is to let doctors and hospitals know whether the author wishes to receive life sustaining medical treatment in the event that he or she is terminally ill or, as a result of accident or illness, is in a state of permanent unconsciousness. Living wills, in varying degrees, are valid in all states.

Making a Valid Will

While most state laws do not expressly provide for a specific will format, all state laws include the minimum elements required for a will to be valid.

In general, in order for a will to be valid, it must:

- be made by a person who has reached the age of majority in his or her state. There are some exceptions to this general rule which we will discuss below;

- be made by a person voluntarily and without pressure from any other person. For this reason, it is not advisable for a potential beneficiary to be present when you instruct your lawyer to draw up your will or indeed to leave any gifts to your lawyer if he or she has drafted your will;

- be made by a person who is of 'sound and disposing mind';

- be in writing (normally);

- be signed by the testator in the presence of two witnesses or, in the case of wills executed in the state of Vermont, three witnesses;

- be signed by all the witnesses in the presence of the testator (after he or she has signed it) and in the presence of each other. A beneficiary under the will or the spouse of such a beneficiary should not act as a witness to the signing of the will. If such a beneficiary or the spouse of such a beneficiary act as a witness, the gift to the beneficiary under the will shall be deemed to be invalid, although the will itself will remain valid;

- include an attestation clause; and

- be notarized if made in the state of Louisiana.

Age of Majority

The age of majority is a legal description that denotes the threshold age at which a person ceases to be a minor and subsequently becomes legally responsible for his or her own actions and decisions. It is the age at which the responsibility of the minor's parents or guardians over them is relinquished. Reaching the age of majority also has a number of important practical consequences for the minor. The minor is now legally entitled to do certain things which he or she could not legally do before. For example, he or she is now legally entitled to enter into binding contracts, hold significant assets, buy stocks and shares, vote in elections, buy and/or consume alcohol, and so on. But more importantly from an estate planning perspective, the minor can now make a will.

It is a general rule in each state that a person must reach the age of majority in their home state before being entitled to make a valid legal will. For details of the age of majority in each state, see Chapter 2.

There are however some exceptions to this general rule. Typically, a person under the age of majority who is already married, or who has been married, is deemed of sufficient age to execute a will. Emancipated minors may also execute a will. An underage person who joins the military or is on active military service can also make a will, as can a seaman or naval officer at sea.

Lastly, and in addition to the above, a court can specifically authorize the making of a will by a minor on application by the minor's parents or guardians. This might be approved, for example, where a minor inherited a large amount of money, invented some innovative computer software or created the next 'You Tube' with some friends. In each case, if the minor is shown to be of a sound disposing capability and the move is deemed prudent, the court will usually consider granting approval for the making of a will by the minor.

Mental Capacity and Undue Influence

In order to make a valid legal will, you must typically be of sound and disposing mind and memory. While what constitutes being of 'sound and disposing mind and memory' differs slightly from state to state, it is generally taken to mean someone who understands:

- what a will is;

- that they are making a will;

- the general extent of their property;

- who their heirs and family members are; and

- the way in which their will proposes to distribute their property (and, of course, to be satisfied with that.)

It is important to note that you need to be of sound mind and memory when you execute your will, not immediately prior to your death. As such, if you end up suffering from any kind of mental impairment late in life such as dementia or Alzheimer's disease, or even from an addiction to drugs or alcohol, the court will look at your mental state at the time you executed your will in order to determine whether it was validly made. If it can be shown that you were not mentally impaired or under the influence at the time you executed your will, the court will most likely deem the will to be valid. If you are suffering from any such impairments, it is advisable that you visit your doctor on the day you execute your will (or even execute it in your doctor's presence) and have your doctor prepare a medical certificate stating that in his or her professional opinion you were mentally competent and lucid at the time you executed your will. These types of statements generally have a strong persuasive effect on the courts, which typically tend to concede mental lucidity in such cases.

Another form of mental incapacity comes under the heading 'undue influence'. Undue influence is the exertion by a third party in a position of trust or authority of any kind of control or influence over another person such that the other person signs a contract or other legal instrument (such as a mortgage or deed) which, absent the influence of the third party, he or she would not ordinarily have signed. A contract or legal instrument may be set aside as being non-binding on any party who signs it while under undue influence.

Claims of undue influence are often raised by sibling beneficiaries in circumstances where one sibling is bequeathed more from a parent than the others. In making your will, you must therefore be careful to avoid potential claims of undue influence where you leave more to one of your children that another. Any such suggestion would give an aggrieved beneficiary the opportunity to attack and try to overturn the terms of your will. In order to reduce the potential likelihood of such claims, it's often useful to document the reasons why you are leaving more to one child than another. Your note can then be attached to your will or at least kept with it.

A second scenario in which claims for undue influence are often raised arises where a testator uses a beneficiary's attorney to draft their will. In such circumstances, aggrieved beneficiaries will, in reliance on that very fact, often assert that the use of the beneficiary's lawyer was evidence of the control the beneficiary had over the testator and the pressure that the beneficiary put on the testator to make the provisions he or she did in the will.

Example of Undue Influence

John constantly visits his uncle Bryan, an 88 year old retired business tycoon, in the nursing home. During his visits, John continuously urges Bryan to leave his vast business interests to him – to the detriment of Bryan's own children who don't visit as often as they should. John, knowing that Bryan is lonely and depressed, threatens to stop visiting him as he is clearly ungrateful for John's kindness and attention. John finally arrives at the nursing home with his lawyer, who has never met Bryan before. John remains present while Bryan instructs the lawyer to write a new will for him in which he purports to leave all his business interest to John.

Ideally, an ethical attorney should never agree to make a will in such circumstances, but in reality, it does happen. Therefore it's always wise to get independent legal advice when you make a will.

Why Make a Will?

There's no legal requirement that anyone should make a will. Rather, it's a privilege our society grants us. But it's also a way of exercising a degree of personal responsibility, and of assisting those who are entitled to some consideration from us. Even for a person with the simplest of circumstances, there really is no good reason not to draft a will.

There are a number of benefits to having a will. In particular, a will:

- allows you to dictate, via clear instructions, how you want your debts settled and assets distributed following your death;

- allows you to choose a representative to wind up your affairs;

- allows you to appoint guardians to take care of your minor children;

- allows you to make property management arrangements to cater for young beneficiaries who will inherit under your will;

- assists in preserving or even enhancing the value of your estate through the incorporation of tax and/or estate planning techniques; and

- gives you peace of mind by allowing you to organize your affairs in a manner that you see fit. This gives you the security of knowing that you haven't left behind a legal and emotional nightmare for your family and friends.

If you don't make a will, a court will make all of the above decisions for you in accordance with the provisions of state law. These decisions may not be in accord with your wishes.

Executors

An executor is the person named in a will to carry out the administration of the deceased's estate in accordance with the provisions of that will. If the deceased failed to make a valid will, or where there is a partial intestacy, the court will appoint a person known as an administrator to wind up the affairs of the deceased in accordance with state intestacy laws. (see page 100)

As we are talking about wills in this chapter, we will focus on the role of executors rather than that of administrators – although in many respects the two roles are very similar.

If you are making a will, you are free to appoint anyone you wish to act as your executor provided they have reached the age of majority in your state. In this regard, you can appoint a relative, a beneficiary under your will, a lawyer or even a bank or professional trustee - the choice is yours. It is also possible to appoint more than one person to act as your executor. Where more than one executor is appointed, these co-executors can act separately (each one with full authority to act on behalf of the estate) or they can be required under the terms of your will to act jointly in which case both executors (or all executors, if there are more than two) must agree to a course of action before taking that action.

Upon your death, your executor will have the legal responsibility and fiduciary duty to handle, safeguard and distribute your property in accordance with the terms of your will. In addition, your executor will also be responsible for procuring the payment of any debts or taxes owing by you or your estate at the date of your death. These debts and taxes, if any, will be paid from your estate (using the assets of the estate) before the distribution of the remainder of the estate's property to the beneficiaries named under your will.

These states use the term "personal representative" instead of "executor"		
Alaska	Maine	North Dakota
Arizona	Michigan	South Carolina
Colorado	Minnesota	South Dakota
Florida	Montana	Utah
Hawaii	Nebraska	Wisconsin
Idaho	New Mexico	

Alternate Executors

When making your will, it's always a good idea to appoint one or more alternate executors. An alternate executor is someone who will perform the duties of the first named executor should they be unable or unwilling to do so (for whatever reason). If the alternate executor is required to act, he or she will be bound by the same legal responsibilities and fiduciary duties as the original executor.

Overview of Executors' Duties

As indicated previously, an executor is the person responsible for carrying out the instructions set out in a will and settling an estate. An executor's duties will usually include locating, collecting, assessing and managing the estate's assets; arranging the discharge of debts and taxes owing by the estate; distributing cash gifts and specific item gifts in accordance with the terms of the testator's will; and entering into appropriate contracts to effect the transfer of real property from the estate to the relevant beneficiary named under the will.

It is also the executor's duty to report the testator's death to insurance companies, banks, and other institutions that might owe money to or hold money on behalf of the estate.

It is common for executors to also be named as trustees of a person's will. In this respect, the testator may establish a testamentary trust for the benefit of certain beneficiaries rather than giving money or assets directly to the beneficiaries. As a trustee, the executor will be responsible for protecting, preserving and investing the trust assets until the time comes to vest those assets in the trust beneficiaries. This usually occurs when the trust beneficiaries reach a certain age or on the occurrence of a specified event.

We'll discuss executor duties further in Chapter 5.

Who Should Be Your Executor?

Choosing an executor is one of the most fundamental tasks associated with making a will. Getting the choice right can mean the difference between a smooth administration on one hand and a tardy administration with unexpected delays and costs on the other hand. It's therefore important to take your time and make the correct choice. Typically, the characteristics to look for in a good executor include good common sense, excellent organizational skills and integrity.

Of course, many people tend to choose their spouse, a sibling, an adult child or a good friend as their executor. Others choose professionals such as a lawyer, accountant or professional trustee. All are good choices provided that the person chosen is both competent and trustworthy.

Other things being equal, it will often pay to choose a family member or friend as executor for the simple reason that these people expect little (if any) compensation in return for their time, will respect your wishes, and are generally keen to process and finalize things as quickly as possible. However, keep in mind that the process can be quite administrative and time is often of the essence. So, you should still ensure that you choose someone who is organizationally reliable and generally up to the task.

It is not enough, however, to simply appoint someone who has all the hallmarks of a good executor. You must actually appoint someone who is willing to take on the role as it is always open for a person to refuse to accept the role despite being nominated in a will. In fact, many often refuse to act as executors because they are either too busy to take on the task or feel daunted by the prospect of doing so.

Important Note

If your chosen executor refuses the appointment, a court will appoint someone to fulfill the role and this person will become known as the "administrator c.t.a." (cum testamento annexo) – meaning an "administrator with the will attached".

For this reason, once you have decided on who you would like to act as your executor, it's important that you actually discuss your choice with them before appointing them in your will. You will need to explain to your proposed executor the nature of his or her role and that it may not be a straight forward and easy process. If, after explaining the role, your nominee is willing to take on the task, then you should be free to formally appoint them under your will.

Executing a Will

State laws set out the formal requirements for executing a will. While these laws are fairly similar in each state, you should still check the specific requirements applicable in your state. In general, however, a 'best practice' guide for executing your will could be summarized as follows:-

- while it is only a legal requirement in the State of Louisiana, you should write your initials, in the presence of two witnesses (in Vermont, you should have three witnesses), at the bottom of each page of your will, except the last (signature) page;

- each of the witnesses should then, in your presence and in the presence of each other, initial each page next to where you just placed your initials;

- you should then insert the date on which you are signing the will in the space provided on the final page of the will;

- you should write your initials beside where you inserted the date;

- each of the witnesses should then, in your presence and in the presence of each other, write their initials beside where you placed your initials (i.e. beside the date);

- you must then sign your ordinary signature, using a pen, in the space provided on the final page; and

- each witness must then, in your presence and in the presence of each other, write his/her name and address in the space provided on the final page of the will and then sign their name with their normal signature.

While the actual execution of your will should be relatively straightforward, there are a number of additional rules which you need to be aware of when executing your will. These rules relate specifically to witnesses and notarization.

In relation to witnesses firstly, they should be at least 18 years of age or older and should not be your spouse or a beneficiary under your will (or a spouse of such beneficiary), as this could nullify any gifts made to them thereunder.

Only in the State of Louisiana must a will be notarized. In all other states notarization is not required — however it is recommended. We have discussed the requirements for notarization above under the heading of self-proving wills and, as such, we will refrain from repeating the information here.

Finally, once you have executed your will, remember to keep it in a safe place. You should also consider informing your executor or even a close family member of friend of the location of your will so that it can be located when needed.

Important Note

Generally, a will must be signed by you or by someone directed to do so on your behalf. Signatures may include marks, initials, a rubber stamp, a 'nick name' or even a former name.

Matters that Can Impact Wills

In drafting your will, it's important to understand that events will most likely occur in your lifetime which will give rise to a need to change the provisions of your will. These events may come around as a result of changes in the law, your financial circumstances, the value of your assets and even in your preferences in relation to beneficiaries. If your will is not updated to address these changes, they can have significant unintended consequences – particularly in respect of the manner in which your assets are ultimately divided amongst your family members.

Some typical changes in circumstances that can cause unintended consequences if not addressed include:

- birth of new family members;

- death of intended beneficiaries;

- significant changes in beneficiaries' circumstances;

- changes in your relationships (such as marriage or divorce);

- acquisition of new assets;

- substantial appreciation in value of particular existing assets; and

- disposal or substantial depreciation in value or loss of certain existing assets.

Important Note

In order to make sure that changes of circumstances are addressed in your will it is recommended that you review and update your will annually or at the very least, every three years. It's also recommended that you review your will on the occurrence of a significant change in your personal circumstances such as in the cases of the examples set out above.

People with sizeable estates (generally those in excess of the estate tax threshold – see Chapter 10) also need to keep an eye on taxes. This is because wills are often used as a method for pre-tax planning, whether in isolation or as part of a broader tax plan. Any change in tax thresholds or the level of particular taxes could have a substantial adverse effect on the potential value of your estate if the terms of your will remain unaltered. It is therefore important to watch for these changes and react accordingly.

No-Contest Clauses

Should you wish to disinherit a child, you should expressly state your intention to do so and include a no-contest clause (see below) in your will. Thereafter, if your will makes no further reference to your child (apart from the statement

of your intention to disinherit), the will effectively disinherits your child. A 'no
-contest' clause is a clause in a will that is designed to threaten to disinherit a
beneficiary of a will if that beneficiary challenges the terms of the will in court.
Where the beneficiary challenges the will, or any provision in it, the clause
triggers a complete and total disinheritance of the beneficiary. An example of a
simple 'no-contest' clause is set out below:

> *"If any person, whether or not related to me by blood or in any way, shall attempt,
> either directly or indirectly, to set aside the probate of my will or oppose or contest
> any of the provisions hereof, then any share or interest in my estate given to that
> person under my will shall be revoked and, in its stead, I give and bequeath the sum
> of one dollar ($1.00), only that, and no further interest whatever in my estate to
> such person."*

The Uniform Probate Code allows for no-contest clauses so long as the person
challenging the will doesn't have probable cause to do so (where the will has
been fraudulently altered, for example).

One thing should be clear; if you decide to disinherit a child or a grandchild
then your will should expressly state your intention to disinherit them. Also, if
you have a child born after your will has been made, the in order to disinherit
them, it will be necessary for you to make a new will or add a codicil to
your existing will. If you do not do so, you run the risk of having your will
successfully challenged.

Challenging a Will

A 'will contest' or 'will challenge' is a legal objection to a will that is usually
initiated by a family member or close relative who feels cheated out of their
rightful inheritance and, as such, wish to challenge the validity of the will in
court.

Generally speaking, only your spouse, children and in some cases grandchildren
have the legal right to inherit from your estate. As such, any challenges to
your will are most likely to emanate from one or more of these parties. Any
challenges to your will are likely to focus on one or more of the following
assertions:

- that you lacked sufficient mental capacity to fully understand what you were doing in making your will;

- that you were subjected to undue influence from a family member or advisor;

- that your will has been fraudulently tampered with;

- that your will has not been properly executed or witnessed in accordance with the law; or

- that the challenger has not been properly provided for under the terms of the will.

If the challenger is ultimately successful, the court will order a re-distribution of your estate based on the determination of court or, where the will is deemed to be invalidly made, in accordance with the rules of intestacy.

Intestacy

When a person dies without a will or if their will cannot be located, is deemed false or invalid (for not meeting the statutory requirements set out above), it is called dying intestate. Every state has statutory rules governing who is entitled to receive a person's property if they die intestate. These rules are commonly known as the 'rules of intestacy' or the 'rules of intestate succession'.

Quite often, the application of the rules of intestacy result in the distribution of a deceased person's property in a manner that they would not have wanted. This is because the rules set out a list of people (known as 'heirs') who are entitled to receive shares in the deceased's property; as well as the order in which they are entitled to receive those shares.

Generally, the rule of thumb an intestacy situation is that the first beneficiaries to receive the deceased's property are the surviving spouse and then the children of the deceased. However, if there is no surviving spouse or children, then the general rule of thumb is that the bigger the estate is, the more distant the relatives who inherit part of it. Such beneficiaries might include the deceased's parents, siblings, grandparents, nieces and nephews, cousins and so on. In those rare cases where no relatives can be found the deceased's property will revert to the state treasury.

Important Note

A partial intestacy occurs where you fail to dispose of your entire estate under your will. In such a case, property not specifically disposed of under your will generally becomes the subject of intestate administration proceedings.

In addition to providing for situations where a person has died without making a will, intestacy laws also apply to situations where a person has failed to deal with all of their property under the terms of their will. This is called a partial intestacy.

Partial intestacy commonly occurs where a will fails to include what's known as a residuary clause. A residuary clause simply provides that any of the deceased's property which has not been specifically gifted under the terms of their will is to be given to a named beneficiary or beneficiaries known as the residuary beneficiary/beneficiaries. A partial intestacy can also occur where the residuary beneficiary or beneficiaries die before the testator and no alternate beneficiaries are named to receive the residue of the estate in their place.

The Main Differences Between Dying "Testate" and "Intestate"?	
Testate	**Intestate**
There is a valid will.	There is no will, or the will is invalid.
The will has been signed by the testator.	There is no will, or the will is invalid.
The estate of the deceased is referred to as a "testate" estate.	The estate of the deceased is referred to as an "intestate" estate.
The person dealing with the winding up of the estate will be known as the "executor of the will" or as the "personal representative".	The person dealing with the winding up of the estate will be known as the "administrator of the estate".
The personal representative will need to file a petition for probate of a will & letters testamentary.	The administrator will need to file a petition for letters of administration.
The person named in the will acts as executor or personal representative.	The administrator will be appointed in accordance with the rule of priority set out under state intestacy law.
The people who receive gifts under a will are called "beneficiaries".	The people who receive distributions on intestacy are called "heirs" or "heirs-at-law".
The beneficiaries are named in the will.	The heirs are determined in accordance with the rules of priority set out under state law.

Where your will is disputed by your heirs or where it is admitted to probate (the legal process of determining the validity of a will and settling the estate), the court will need to satisfy itself that it is valid. To this end, it will look at issues such as your age and mental capacity at the time you made your will, whether there might have been any undue influence, as well as the manner in which the will was signed and executed. If all of these matters are in order, then the will should be admitted to probate.

However, there are situations where valid wills might not be admitted to probate. This typically happens where the will is not admitted to probate within the time frame set out by state law (usually 30 days following the death of the testator). Where this happens, there is a real risk that the court might declare the will null and void; and order that the deceased's estate be distributed according to the laws of intestacy.

Apportionment and Distribution of Assets on Intestacy

While intestacy laws generally vary from state to state, this variance has been greatly lessened by the Uniform Probate Code (which has been adopted by 18 states in full and by numerous states in part). The Code provides a good example of the rules relating to the distribution of assets on intestacy. However, you should check your own state law for a more thorough understanding of the rules applicable in your state.

Important Note

The intestacy laws which will apply to the distribution of a deceased person's assets will usually be the laws applicable in the deceased's state of residence.

Under the Code, priority of inheritance is given to the following persons in the following order:

- surviving spouse;

- descendents (children, grandchildren, etc.);

- parents;

- descendents of deceased's parents (siblings, nieces and nephews);

- grandparents; and

- descendents of grandparents (aunts, uncles and cousins).

Under the Code, relatives are each apportioned a certain percentage of the deceased's estate. The percentages are as follows:

Share of Surviving Spouse

The share of a surviving spouse is calculated as follows:-

- A surviving spouse is entitled to the entire estate if neither the deceased's descendants (i.e. children, grandchildren and great grandchildren) nor the deceased's parents have survived the deceased.

- If the deceased's parents survive but no descendents survive the deceased, the surviving spouse is entitled to the first $200,000 of the estate plus ¾ of anything exceeding that amount.

- If the deceased is survived by a spouse and descendants from that marriage only, the surviving spouse will take the first $150,000 of the estate plus ½ of anything exceeding that amount, plus all community property.

- If the deceased is survived by descendents from the marriage to the surviving spouse and by descendents from someone other than his or her surviving spouse, the surviving spouse takes the first $100,000 of the estate plus ½ of anything exceeding that amount, plus all community property.

Share of Descendents

- If the deceased's spouse does not survive the deceased and the deceased's descendants do, then the deceased's descendents take the entire estate.

- In some cases, if the deceased's child has predeceased the deceased, that child's surviving children will inherit their parent's share of the intestate estate. This is known as 'per stirpes' distribution.

Share of Parents

- If the deceased is not survived by a spouse or descendents, his or her entire net estate passes to his or her parents equally or, if only one survives, to the survivor.

Share of Other Relatives

- If neither the deceased's spouse, descendents, nor parents survive the deceased, the entire net estate passes to the deceased's siblings. If there are no siblings or no descendents of the deceased's siblings, the deceased's estate goes to any surviving grandparents or their descendents.

Do-It-Yourself Wills

While you can easily obtain will forms and other legal document forms in a 'fill-in-the-blanks' format online or from various stores, we recommend that you take extreme care in determining which forms to use and which to ignore. Your personal, financial and other circumstances will grow in complexity as you age and, as such, your changing needs might not be sufficiently addressed by a 'one-size fits all' form. This will apply particularly where you have a very large estate such as one which exceeds the value of the current estate tax thresholds (see Chapter 10) or where you have complex business and financial interests.

However, if your estate is 'normal' then, in many cases, these documents can suffice. For example, if a husband and wife wished to leave everything to each other in the event of their death, or in the event that both died at the same time, to their children, a 'do-it-yourself will' can suffice. This is because the distributions are relatively straightforward. Similarly, if you simply wish to make normal gifts (real estate, cash, art, etc) to your family and friends, these types of wills are also generally fine.

Yet it can happen that the use of sub-standard "do-it-yourself wills" leads to confusion in the interpretation of your will, delays in distributions being made and unwanted tax consequences. In one well-known case, a do-it-yourself testator wrote "I leave all my personal property to my wife." Endless chaos ensued because the law distinguishes 'real property' (land and real estate) from 'personal property' (all property other than land and real estate, but including leasehold property, such as cash, antiques, etc). Here the bulk of the estate was in the form of freehold land, which on a literal reading was simply not dealt with under the will, and could have been split between various relatives upon intestacy. In this particular case the widow had to go through the trauma, delay, and considerable expense of seeking a declaration that her husband intended her to inherit his real estate, as well as his personal estate! (The testator's personal estate in the case in point was not of great value.)

 Warning

While all of Enodare's legal documents are drafted to a very high standard, we have no way of knowing whether they are suitable for you having regard to your particular circumstances. As such, you still need to use these documents with care as the decision to use them is up to you. If you are in any doubt as to their suitability for you, speak to an attorney.

If you are happy to draft a do-it-yourself will, we recommend that you carefully consider the use of such a document in the context of your overall situation and personal circumstances. Where you have any doubt or concern as to the suitability of a particular document to your circumstances, you should consult an estate-planning lawyer before you sign. It's the best way to ensure you don't end up with messy, unintended consequences. The price you'll pay for peace of mind — and the assurance that those you want to inherit will inherit — will be more than worth it.

Do I Need a Lawyer?

The short answer is "no." In every state, citizens are free to draft their will on their own, without legal representation. If your situation is not a complicated one, and you simply want to make gifts, appoint guardians and executors etc under your will, then preparing your own will should not be very difficult provided that you have some good self-help materials to hand. But as with the do-it-yourself kits, if your situation is complex or is unusual in some way, you should, at the very least, consult an attorney.

 Resources

1) **Book**: Make Your Own Last Will & Testament - See page 266.

2) **Online Software:** Make Your Will Online - See page 270.

3) **CD Software:** Will Writer - See page 268.

CHAPTER 5:
EXECUTORS & PROBATE

Chapter Overview

This chapter will give you an overview of the obligations and responsibilities of your executor as well as a general understanding of the probate process.

Chapter 5

CHAPTER 5

EXECUTORS & PROBATE

What Is an Executor?

As already mentioned in Chapter 4, an executor is a person appointed under the terms of your will for the purpose of winding up your estate and distributing your property in accordance with the terms of that will.

The role of executor is both important and difficult. Your executor must be prepared to carry out the sometimes wide-ranging, sometimes minimal, steps required to finalize every aspect of your estate. More often than not, the probate of your estate will require much more from your executor than simply writing checks and giving your beneficiaries their gifts from your estate. The process can be a demanding and time-consuming task involving complicated taxes, fee payments, disputes amongst beneficiaries, and tricky asset transfers. It is therefore important that you appoint an executor capable of navigating the sometimes treacherous waters of probate and estate administration.

What Is Probate?

Before we delve further into the role of your executor, we'll have a brief look at the probate process. Probate, in short, is the process by which your property is transferred to the beneficiaries named in your will after your death and is usually carried out under court supervision. If you have not made a will and die intestate, the process is still guided by state law and court supervision. However, the comparable process is known as intestate administration.

Every state has its own set of probate laws (often codified in a probate code) which set out the specific rules and procedures for probate in that state. At a minimum, these laws typically stipulate the requirements for a valid will, tell us who is going to administer the estate, tell us who is entitled to receive assets from the estate, identify which creditors need to be paid upon the deceased's death and in what order of priority, and determine how to distribute the balance of the deceased's assets after the payment of all taxes and debts of the estate.

Each state has its own set of specific procedures which must be followed when bringing an estate to probate. In most cases, the procedure is the same. Generally, your executor's first task will be to locate your will. Of course, without a will, probate cannot take place. It is for this reason that it is recommend that, upon appointment, you provide your executor with details of where your will can be located when the time comes - e.g. in a safe deposit box, in your lawyers office etc. Once located, your executor should try to determine whether your will is valid 'on its face' by ensuring, for example, that it has been signed by you and witnessed by the correct number of witnesses. Most states require a will to be witnessed by two witnesses (in Vermont, three witnesses are required). Your executor must also determine that the located will is in fact your last will as only your last will has any legal effect.

Next, if your will is in legal order, your executor must determine whether probate is required and, if so, file your will in the probate court and apply for probate. This simply means that your executor sets in motion the process of legally proving the validity of your will and obtaining the consent of the court to wind up your affairs. Whether probate is required or not depends on the laws of your state. In some states, probate is required for all estate. In others, however, estates with a small monitory value will not need to go through the probate process or, alternatively, can avail of a more streamlined procedure for wining up the estate.

Once an application for probate has been made, it is the Probate Court's job to formally rule upon the validity of your will (quite often this is just a rubber-stamp affair). However, the court must wait a specific period of time before doing so to allow any challengers to your will (or part thereof) to file their objection. Any such challenges must be made within a specified timeframe (which changes from state to state, so your executor will need to check the notice and timing requirements for your particular state).

Once the court deems the will valid, and accepts your executor's appointment as executor, your executor may begin to pay taxes, settle debts and other claims against your estate and, when this is done, distribute the estate's assets to your beneficiaries. If the will is invalid, your executor will need to proceed as if you died intestate. In which case, the court will appoint an administrator to administer the estate. This may or may not be the executor you have chosen in your will depending on state law.

Finally, the last step of the process occurs when your executor finalizes your estate by filing the necessary papers and accounts with the court. These must include an accounting of assets that formed part of the estate; details of what was paid out from the estate (and why); as well as copies of any notices and tax returns issued, received or filed, as the case may be, by the estate. Your executor will be expected to provide proof of distribution of your assets to the correct beneficiaries, usually by providing signed receipts from the beneficiaries. Also included may be copies of deeds signed by your executor for the transfer of real property, and instruments of distribution for any of your personal property.

As soon as the court recognizes that your executor has successfully completed all the steps necessary to administer your estate, he or she will be released from further service as executor of your estate. and your estate will be closed.

Who Can Be Your Executor?

In practice, you are more or less free to appoint anyone you wish to act as your executor – subject to a few exceptions. Normally, a person will not be able to act as an executor if they are under the age of majority in their state of residence, if they have been convicted of a felony, or are not a U.S. citizen.

In addition, certain states prohibit people residing outside that state from acting as executors unless insurance bonds are first put in place. As such, if you are planning on appointing an out-of-state resident as your executor, you should check your state laws to see if a bond is required. The cost of any such bond will be borne by your estate.

An Overview of an Executor's Duties, Powers and Risks

While it is not within the scope of this book to provide a comprehensive discussion on executor duties, it is useful for you to have a general understanding of those duties so that you can decide who is best for the role.

In essence, an executor will have two types of duties – procedural duties and fiduciary duties. Procedural duties are actions that the executor must perform to bring the estate through probate. Fiduciary duties, on the other hand, are duties that the executor owes to the beneficiaries of the estate whose assets the executor has control over.

Once the executor has applied for probate, he or she will have the following procedural duties and responsibilities:

- notifying beneficiaries named in the will;

- drafting and arranging publication in a newspaper of a notice to creditors; and sending a copy of that notice (by mail) to each creditor that the executor knows of;

- sending copies of the deceased's official death notice to the post office, utility companies, banks and credit card companies;

- locating and safeguarding assets;

- inventorying assets and having them appraised and valued;

- collecting all moneys owing to the estate;

- checking with the deceased's employer for any unpaid salary and benefits that might be owing to the estate;

- filing for outstanding social security, civil service, veteran and other benefits;

- filing claims for life insurance benefits;

- filing state death tax and federal estate tax returns;

- paying out valid and proven claims against the estate; and

- distributing all remaining assets to the beneficiaries.

An executor also owes your estate and its beneficiaries a fiduciary duty arising from his or her position as executor. A fiduciary duty arises where a person undertakes to act for and on behalf of another in relation to a particular matter and in circumstances which give rise to a relationship of trust and confidence between the parties. A fiduciary duty is a legal one and breach of that duty gives rise to a cause of action against the fiduciary. (i.e the executor)

The main fiduciary duties that your executor will have include the duty to:

- adhere strictly to the terms of the will and to your intentions;

- keep estate assets separate from other assets;

- keep accurate records and accounts of the estate's dealings;

- provide information to the beneficiaries named in your will in a timely manner;

- administer the estate with the same due care and skill that a person of ordinary prudence would exercise in dealing with his or her own property;

- administer the estate in the best interests of the beneficiaries and not in the executor's self interest; and

- avoid conflicts of interest, whether actual or perceived.

Powers of an Executor

Until termination of his or her appointment, your executor will have the same power over the title to your property as you would ordinarily have. However, this power is exercisable in trust for the benefit of your creditors and beneficiaries.

In addition, executors are afforded a variety of additional powers under state law. These include powers to:

- employ persons for the purpose of valuing assets and evaluating the liabilities of the estate;

- receive a defined level of compensation or a reasonable level of compensation in return for acting as executor of the estate;

- petition the court for an order determining the validity of a will, the entitlement of beneficiaries to claim under the will, approving the final accounting of the estate as prepared by the executor and the plan of distribution of the estate assets;

- distribute the estate's assets; and

- close the probate of the estate.

In addition to the powers granted under state law, executors tend to be afforded further powers under the terms of a will. These additional powers are given to the executor to allow him manage the testator's estate. Typically, the larger the estate the greater the extent of the powers given to executors.

Executor's Liability

As with any position of responsibility, there are potential personal liabilities that come with your executor's role. We have set out below some examples (but not an exhaustive list) of ways in which an executor may be held liable for a breach of duty or responsibility.

Your executor can be held liable (civilly and/or criminally) if he or she:

- violates any applicable law;

- fails to comply with the terms of your will;

- abuses any of his or her powers as executor;

- deals in the estate assets for his or her own account;

- causes unreasonable delay in administering the estate;

- causes loss, damage or devaluation of any assets;

- takes action without appropriate approval, including those actions that require the consent of the estate's beneficiaries, the prior approval of co-executors or a court; and

- fails to make any payment or secure any debt.

Further, while executors are empowered to seek advice before making investment decisions, the ability to make these decisions is personal to the executor and cannot be delegated. Any improper delegation of executor duties or responsibilities, such as allowing investment advisors complete discretion to make decisions on behalf of the estate's investments, can open the door to liability for both restitution and damages. If your executor is found guilty of a breach of his or her duties or responsibilities, the court can require the executor to compensate the estate for the amount of any loss suffered by it. The compensation amount is often referred to as a "surcharge".

Protecting Your Executor from Liability

If someone agrees to perform as your executor, you should see to it that they are protected from liability and return their last, generous act of friendship.

There are a number of ways that you can ensure that your executor is protected. While some of these ways need to be provided for in your will, others need to be implemented before your death.

Protection Under the Terms of Your Will

The terms of your will can be drafted in a manner so as to reduce the chance of your executor being exposed to personal liability in circumstances where he or she acts diligently and in good faith in the carrying out of his or her duties. By way of simple example, your will could authorize your executor to manage a particular business activity that was somewhat risky and, in conjunction with doing that, could provide that the executor will not be held liable for any loss to the value of that business where he or she acts in good faith. The rationale for the inclusion of such clauses is relatively straight forward. In the absence of including these exclusion clauses, your executor would most likely abstain from taking on any involvement in the management of such assets in circumstances where he or she could find himself or herself being sued personally for any subsequent loss – even where the executor did all he or she could humanly do! These clauses allow executors to get on with the business at hand while at the same time ensuring that they still act with due care and attention in the performance of their duties.

Obtain the Consent of Beneficiaries

Another way in which your executor can reduce the possibility of personal liability is to obtain the written permission of all concerned beneficiaries before taking a particular course of action or the carrying out certain activities, for example the sale of real estate investments. This consent can be obtained by you before you die or by your executor after you die.

While it's not vital, the written consent should expressly state that the beneficiaries will not hold the executor liable if they carry out the approved action(s). The mere existence of such a written approval would make it exceptionally difficult for beneficiaries to subsequently take a successful action against the executor for losses to the estate incurred from the carrying out of the approved activities (unless of course the executor was negligent in carrying out the activities approved by the beneficiaries).

Take Out an Executor's Insurance Bond

One of the best protections available to executors in the current market is insurance cover. The estate and/or the executor can take out executor insurance in the form of a surety bond, obtainable from most insurance companies. The bond protects both beneficiaries and creditors from losses suffered by the estate due to neglect or omission by the executor. Although a bond is not always required, beneficiaries may request it (simply if they feel it is necessary) and even the probate court might request it from time to time. Needless to say, while it protects the estate, it also protects the executor from personal liability as he or she is afforded monetary protection up to the value of the insurance bond. The value of the bond should, in most cases, equate to the full value of the estate. The premium for the bond will be payable by the estate.

You can expressly require the executor to take out such a bond under the terms of your will. The costs of the bond will be borne by your estate.

Obtain the Consent of the Probate Court

Finally, where an executor is uncertain as to how to proceed in a particular situation, he or she may apply to court for directions on how to proceed. Having considered the issue, the court will direct the executor on how best to proceed in the circumstances. This direction will be given in the form of a court order. Where the executor follows the directions of the court order to the letter, it would be extremely difficult for a beneficiary to take action personally against the executor given that he is carrying out actions sanctioned by the court. Of course, if the court was not aware of all the facts in the case, the executor would not be adequately protected in this instance.

Compensating Your Executor

You can draft your will to pay your executor a fixed fee, an hourly fee, a statutory fee or no fee at all. Should you choose a fixed or flat fee, you simply write that fee into the will in a compensation clause. Most states have a statutorily defined "reasonable rate of compensation" for executors (and trustees). This rate is sometimes a percentage of the net value of the estate, e.g. 2.5%.

Often, if you appoint a close friend, relative or family member, you can pre-arrange that they will serve their appointment for free. However, remember that probating an estate is a time-consuming and difficult task. So, if you are able, you may wish to compensate your executor, at least nominally.

If you draft your will so as to refuse or overly limit compensation to your executor, we recommend that you include an exemption for professional services, e.g. banks, lawyers etc. Professionals most often will not serve without compensation and will therefore insist on charging their professional rates to the estate.

CHAPTER 6:
POWERS OF ATTORNEY

Chapter Overview

A power of attorney is a very important and very powerful tool. In this chapter we define and explain the role of a power of attorney in your estate plan.

Chapter 6

CHAPTER 6

POWERS OF ATTORNEY

What Is a Power of Attorney?

A power of attorney is a legal document by which you can appoint and authorize another person (usually a trusted friend, family member, colleague or adviser) to act on your behalf and to legally bind you in that respect. While most people fail to see the importance of having a power of attorney, there are many compelling reasons why they should be used. Suppose, for example that:

- you are going to be out of the country for an extended period, and need someone trustworthy to manage your business affairs while you're away;

- you wish to acquire property in another state, and you need to authorize a local to sign and lodge documents on your behalf;

- you want someone to manage your real estate for you; or

- you're getting a little bit older and wish to appoint someone you know and trust to make healthcare decisions on your behalf should the day come when you are unable to do so yourself.

A power of attorney can be used to facilitate your needs in each of these scenarios.

The person giving the power of attorney is referred to as the 'donor', 'grantor' or 'principal', while the recipient is called the 'agent', 'attorney-in-fact' or just plain 'attorney' (which doesn't mean they have to be a legal practitioner!).

Types of Powers of Attorney

There are a number of different types of power of attorney all serving different needs and requirements. We'll take a look at some of the main types below.

General Power of Attorney

A 'general power of attorney' is virtually <u>unlimited</u> in scope. It allows your agent to act as your authorized legal representative in relation to the whole cross-section of your legal and financial affairs, until such time as that authorization is terminated. In other words, your agent will have full legal authority to make decisions and take actions on your behalf, as if you were taking them yourself. This could, for example, include signing letters and checks, executing contracts, etc!

While you cannot generally limit the scope of the power conferred under a general power of attorney, there are nonetheless some presumed limits to the agent's authority. For example, your agent is not normally permitted to assume any position or office that you might hold, such as the position of employee, company director, trustee, personal representative or indeed many others. Furthermore, an agent cannot execute a will on your behalf (or amend an existing one), take action concerning your marriage or delegate his or her authorization under your power of attorney to a third party, unless expressly authorized to do so in the power of attorney document. An attorney is also prevented from making gifts of your assets, other than small gifts that you yourself might have been expected to make having regard to the size of your estate.

It's important to bear in mind that you will remain personally liable for the actions of your agent, so you should grant authorization only to someone you trust implicitly.

A general power of attorney (unless stated to be durable) automatically comes to an end if you become mentally incapacitated or die.

Limited Power of Attorney

A 'limited power of attorney' is very similar to a general power of attorney except that it imposes specific and sometimes substantial limits upon the authorization granted to your agent. This could, for example, be a limit to the scope or duration of the authority granted to him.

Often, people granting powers of attorney limit their agent's authority to completing specific transactions or tasks. For example, you may appoint someone as your agent solely for the purpose of having them sign a document on your behalf but only in a format pre-approved by you and attached to the power of attorney document itself. Alternatively, you can appoint your agent for the sole purpose of dealing with a single task or transaction (such as the sale of a piece of real estate to a specified individual at a specified price). These types of limitations remove a substantial part of the risk associated with granting powers of attorney.

Similar to the position with a general power of attorney, you will remain personally liable for the actions of your agent. In addition, a limited power of attorney (unless stated to be durable) will automatically come to an end if you become mentally incapacitated or die.

Healthcare Power of Attorney

One of the most common forms of power of attorney in use today is the 'medical' or 'healthcare' power of attorney ("HCPOA").

A HCPOA allows you to authorize an agent to make healthcare decisions on your behalf should you be incapacitated and unable to do so. The authorization conferred on your agent can cover any form of healthcare decision and applies even where you are not terminally ill or permanently unconscious. It also applies in cases of temporary unconsciousness (if you were in an accident, for instance) or in case of mental diseases like Alzheimer's disease which affects the decision-making process. The important point to remember is that it does not automatically terminate if you become incapacitated – in other words, it's durable!

With a HCPOA, you can specify guidelines and directions regarding the medical treatment that you want to receive during any period in which you are unable to make healthcare decisions on your own behalf. Save in the most extreme cases, your agent will be obliged to follow these instructions. You can also give your agent full freedom to make healthcare decisions on your behalf during any period in which you are incapacitated.

Ordinary and Durable Powers of Attorney

Apart from the above types of powers of attorney, powers of attorney can be categorized as either being ordinary or durable - both of which come to an end when the principal dies.

An ordinary power of attorney is only valid for as long as the principal is capable of making decisions and acting for him or herself. If the principal dies or becomes mentally incapacitated, the power of attorney is deemed invalid and immediately ceases to have effect. As a result, the family of the principal may be left in a position whereby they are powerless to deal with the principal's affairs unless they seek court intervention.

A durable power of attorney, on the other hand, remains valid even if the principal later becomes mentally incapacitated. In fact, the continuing validity of the agent's authorization after the principal becomes incapacitated is the significant difference between ordinary and durable powers of attorney.

To be recognized as durable, a power of attorney should contain a clear and unambiguous statement to the effect that it is intended to be 'durable'. It should also state that 'this power of attorney shall not be affected by the subsequent incapacity of the principal' or 'this power of attorney shall become effective upon the incapacity of the principal', as the case may be, or else use similar words that show it was intended to be valid even after the principal became incapacitated.

Springing Powers of Attorney

A 'springing' power of attorney is one that becomes effective at a future time. In other words, it 'springs' into effect when a defined event occurs, typically the incapacity of the principal.

Like most durable powers of attorney, it will contain a clause that provides that the principal's doctor will need to determine whether he or she is competent to handle his/her financial affairs before the authority will come into effect.

Once it comes into effect, a springing power of attorney will continue until the principal's death, or until revoked by the court.

Mutual Powers of Attorney

Mutual powers of attorney are generally made between a husband and wife, and occasionally between the members of smaller businesses or professional firms. They serve as indicators of the mutual trust, confidence and the reliance that the parties enjoy within their relationship.

Each spouse or partner will appoint the other (or others) as their agent so as to ensure that their joint plans are implemented in the unfortunate event that one of them is rendered unable to act by illness or injury.

Cascading Powers of Attorney

A cascading power of attorney is simply a form of power of attorney which allows for the appointment of alternative or substitute agents or attorneys-in-fact. Its purpose is to provide for a backup in the situation where the first agent is unable or unwilling to act, and then further backups to replace the alternative attorneys-in-fact if they, too, decline to act, or cannot act for any reason.

Capacity to Make a Power of Attorney

Generally, anyone who has reached the age of majority in their state, who has sufficient mental capacity and who is not an un-discharged bankrupt can make a power of attorney. Even a company or a partnership can make a power of attorney.

The precise requirements for making a power of attorney differ from state to state. As such, if you are in any doubt as to whether you can make a power of attorney, you should seek the advice of a practicing attorney in your state.

What Does "Being Incapable or Incapacitated" Mean?

You will be deemed to be 'incapable' or 'incapacitated' if you are unable to understand and process information that is relevant to making an informed decision and if you are also unable to evaluate the likely consequences of making that decision.

The decision as to who determines whether you are incapacitated or not is generally set out in your power of attorney. Generally, a power of attorney will state that two doctors or attending physicians must agree that you are incapable before you are actually deemed incapacitated and your power of attorney comes into effect.

While it may be somewhat obvious, it's worth pointing out that you must be mentally capable of granting a power of attorney at the time when the document was signed. This generally means that you must, if required, show that you are aware of the nature and extent of your assets and personal circumstances and that you understand your obligations in relation to your dependants and the nature of the power being granted to the agent under the power of attorney.

If you are found to be incapable or incapacitated in a time where you believe you are not, you have the right to request a capacity review hearing for the purpose of affirming or quashing that determination. You will have the right to be represented by counsel at that hearing. Agents appointed under a power of attorney have a general duty to explain this right to you and cannot try to prevent you from contacting a lawyer or asking for a review hearing. This said, it should be remembered that unless the agent is a professional accustomed to acting under a power of attorney, the likelihood is that the agent will not be aware of his obligation in this regard.

Should I Make a Power of Attorney?

The simple answer is yes! If you have an income or property of any description it's a good idea to execute a durable power of attorney especially if you believe that health problems may make it impossible for you to handle your personal financial affairs in the future. Even if you have no impending health issues, you should still have a durable power of attorney in case you, because of an accident or sudden illness, ever become unable to make decisions for yourself.

Have you ever considered what would happen if:-

- you were involved in a serious accident, which left you in a coma. What would your family do, in both the short and the longer term, if they had no power to access your bank accounts or take care of your business affairs?

- you began to have blackouts, and act in an out-of-character fashion. You're diagnosed as having a brain tumor, and before long you lose the capacity to function normally, or make rational decisions. Will your property, financial and other affairs be stuck in limbo?

In both of these cases, a durable power of attorney would be of great assistance to you. During your period of incapacity, your agent would be in a position to manage the many practical and financial tasks that may arise. For example, bills will need to be paid, bank deposits will need to be made, and someone will need to handle insurance and benefits paperwork, ...etc.

Many other matters may need attention as well, ranging from handling property repairs and lettings to managing investments or even a small business. In most cases, a durable general power of attorney is the best way to take care of all these and other similar tasks.

In addition, by preparing a power of attorney now, you can ensure that a person of your choosing will manage your property, assets and affairs rather than a court appointed conservator.

What Happens Without a Power of Attorney?

If you don't make a durable power of attorney, someone may have to be formally appointed by a court to make financial and other practical decisions (other than medical decisions) on your behalf. In essence, your family will have to make an application to court to have it make a determination that you cannot take care of your own affairs and request the court to make an order appointing a 'conservator' (also known as a guardian of the estate, committee, or curator) on your behalf. This application is often made in public and, in some instances, a notice of the intended application may even be published in a local newspaper. This can, as you will appreciate, be quite embarrassing and intrusive. Moreover, if family members disagree over who is to be appointed as the conservator or guardian, the proceedings may well become even more disagreeable and drawn out. The longevity of the proceedings can substantially increase the costs, especially as lawyers will need to be hired.

While the court will usually appoint a close family member to act as your conservator, it is under no obligation to do so. As such, it could end up appointing a complete stranger - someone who does not know you, who is not aware of your wishes, and who can legally ignore your family's requests and needs! For this reason alone, and forgetting the cost of such appointments, conservatorships are best avoided.

A conservator will generally need to:

- post a bond (a type of insurance policy) in case he or she steals or misuses your property;

- prepare (or hire a lawyer or accountant to prepare) detailed financial reports and periodically file them with the court; and

- get court approval before carrying out certain transactions, such as selling real estate or making investments.

The cost of these items all add up making conservatorships an expensive process; a process which ultimately needs to be paid from your estate. Appointing an agent under your power of attorney is, when done right, far more flexible and cheaper than a conservatorship and therefore an often favored alternative.

What If You Don't Think You Need a Power of Attorney?

You may not think that you need a durable power of attorney if, for example, you are married or if you have put the majority of your property and possessions into a living trust (also known as a family or inter vivos trust) or if you hold property as a joint tenant. However, the reality is that in all three of these instances, you will still need a durable general power of attorney if you become incapacitated.

Marriage

If you are married, your spouse will have a good degree of authority to deal with the property that you own together - for example, he or she will be able to continue to pay bills from a joint bank account or sell stocks or shares held in a joint brokerage account. However, there are very real restrictions on your spouse's ability to sell property owned by both of you. For example, in many states, one spouse cannot sell jointly owned real estate or automobiles without the consent of the other. If the other spouse is incapacitated and cannot give this consent, the sale cannot proceed. This may have important effects, particularly where the sales proceeds are required to pay on-going medical expenses or other important expenses.

In addition, when it comes to property in which your spouse has no legal interest, he or she will have no legal authority to deal with your assets in the absence of a durable power of attorney or court order.

Living Trusts

Even where you have a living trust, you should still consider making a power of attorney. In the majority of cases, the 'successor trustee' appointed under your living trust to distribute the trust property after your death also has the authority to take over management of the trust property during any period in which you become incapacitated. However, given that most people don't transfer all of their property into a living trust, a power of attorney should be made to cover any such property that's not so transferred.

For more information on living trusts, see Chapter 9.

Joint Tenancy

Joint tenancy is a form of joint ownership where each co-owner holds an undivided interest in the subject property. When one of the co-owners dies, the remaining co-owners automatically inherit the deceased's share of the property. While matters are relatively straight-forward in the case of death, they can become more complicated where one of the joint tenants becomes incapacitated. This is because the other joint tenants will have limited authority to deal with the joint tenancy property in the absence of being able to procure the consent of the incapacitated joint tenant. Real estate provides a good example of such a problem. If one owner becomes incapacitated, the others have no legal authority to sell or refinance the incapacitated owner's share of the property. By contrast, if the incapacitated joint owner had a durable power of attorney in place, they could give their agent authority to deal with their share of joint tenancy property and all matters relating to same, such as bank accounts, insurance and litigation. This would at least provide a means by which the assets could be legally dealt with and the rights of the co-owner exercised or enforced.

The Relationship Between Principal and Agent

One of the principal features underlying the relationship between a principal and an agent is the requirement that the agent acts with the utmost good faith on behalf of the principal. It is a relationship built on trust in which the agent is obliged to act with loyalty on behalf of the principal and in accordance with instructions received from the principal. The agent can neither intentionally ignore these instructions nor negligently act in the performance of them. In return for this loyalty, a principal instills confidence and trust in the agent thereby creating a fiduciary relationship of trust and confidence between the parties. It is this relationship of trust and confidence that underlies every specific action taken, or left untaken by the agent.

Unfortunately, human nature being what it is, the principles of trust upon which the fiduciary relationship is built are often honored more on paper than in observance. The reality is that people sometimes succumb to the pressure of other affairs, to a lack of thought about and appreciation of their obligations, and of course to temptation. This risk of breach is the primary risk associated with agency relationships particularly because of the agent's ability to bind the principal.

Who Can Be an Agent?

While there is no need for an agent to be a lawyer or other professional person, he or she must be an adult capable of making decisions and carrying out specific tasks on your behalf. What's more, if the specific power of attorney you intend to create is one for healthcare, it may be advisable to weigh the agent's capacity for compassion as more valuable in this instance than their talents as a financial analyst or businessman.

The agent cannot be an un-discharged bankrupt and should not be the owner, operator or employee of a nursing home or extended care facility in which the principal is resident. Neither can the agent be a witness to your signature on the power of attorney.

Joint or Joint and Independent Agents

Sometimes a principal will want to appoint one or more agents to act on his/her behalf. Where the principal makes such a decision, he or she needs to decide whether the agents will be 'joint' agents or 'joint and independent' agents.

Joint agents must act together. As such, they must unanimously agree on a course of action before that action can proceed. Furthermore, in taking any action, joint agents must take the same action at the same time. For instance, if one of the agents is missing or unwilling to engage in a specific action, the remaining agents are powerless to act. This type of arrangement adds a degree of protection to the principal as it removes the possibility of any of the agents acting outside their instructions or in a 'rogue' capacity. 'Joint and independent' agents, on the other hand, can act either together or individually. As such, while both or all agents may be acting on behalf of the same principal and in relation to the same matter, they will not be obligated to consult with each other before taking an action which can bind the principal.

In the ordinary course, it is recommended that you avoid appointing joint agents. Rather, if more than one is to be appointed, it is preferable to appoint agents as alternates to the original agent.

Alternate Agents

While it is not necessary to do so, it is always a very good idea to appoint an alternate agent (also known as a substitute agent). The authority conferred on an alternate agent will only come into effect where the primary agent is unable or unwilling to act on behalf of the principal. In such circumstances, the alternate agent will acquire full power to act (unless expressly restricted) under the power of attorney.

In many cases, third parties (particularly financial institutions) will require proof that the original agent is unable or unwilling to act as agent under the power of attorney before accepting instructions from the alternate agent. In such cases, it's often useful for an alternate agent to request a signed confirmation from the principal revoking the authority of the original agent or, if available, from the original agent confirming in writing his or her refusal or inability to act as agent.

Scope of an Agent's Powers

Depending on whether the power of attorney is general or limited in nature, your agent will have as many or as few powers as the principal specifies in the power of attorney. Within the scope of the authority you confer on your agent he or she can do anything that you can legally do.

You can give your agent authority to do some or all of the following:

    (i)   use your assets to discharge the day-to-day expenses of you and your family;

    (ii)   purchase, sell, lease, let, maintain, repair, pay taxes on and mortgage real estate and other property;

    (iii)   claim and collect social insurance, government, civil, military and other entitlements;

(iv)   invest money in stocks, bonds and mutual funds;

(v)   effect transactions with financial institutions;

(vi)   buy, maintain and sell insurance policies and annuities;

(vii)   file and discharge your tax liabilities;

(viii)   operate your small business;

(ix)   claim real estate or other property that you inherit or are otherwise entitled to;

(x)   transfer property into a trust you've created (if the rules of the trust permit);

(xi)   engage someone to represent you in court or to run legal actions on your behalf; and

(xii)   manage your affairs generally.

Note that the above list is not exhaustive.

Duties and Responsibilities of an Agent

Generally speaking, your agent has the following primary duties and responsibilities:

- to act in your best interest;

- to keep accurate records of dealings and transactions undertaken on your behalf;

- to act towards you with the utmost good faith and to avoid situations where there is a conflict of interest; and

- to keep your property and money separate from their own.

As far as keeping accurate records is concerned, the agent should keep a list or register of:

- all the principal's assets as at the date of his first transaction;

- all assets acquired and disposed of and the date and particulars of each such transaction;

- all receipts and disbursements and the date and particulars of each such transaction;

- all investments bought and sold and the date and particulars of each such transaction;

- all the principal's liabilities as of the date of the agent's first transaction;

- all liabilities incurred and paid and the date and particulars of each such transaction; and

- all compensation taken by the agent and the manner in which it was calculated.

Your agent should keep these records until he or she ceases acting for you and until the date upon which he or she is relieved from acting as your agent. These records should be handed over to either the agent's successor, or if the power of attorney terminates by reason of the principal's death, to the principal's legal personal representative. Of course, if the principal has merely recovered from an incapacity, the records can be given back to the principal directly.

Choosing an Agent

Your agent will be acting on your behalf, as such, the person you choose should obviously be someone you know and trust thoroughly. In making any decisions, you must bear in mind that your agent will have complete authority to deal with your financial and legal affairs (subject to any limitations or restrictions specified in your power of attorney).

You should ensure that the person you choose has adequate financial management skills and sufficient time to handle your affairs properly. Your agent must be available when required, be able to objectively make decisions and be able to keep accurate financial records.

What Laws Govern My Power of Attorney?

A power of attorney is normally governed by the law specified in the document itself or by the law of the jurisdiction in which the actions of the agent are to be performed. Normally, this is the place in which the property or assets of the principal are located. For this reason, it makes sense to appoint an agent located in that specific jurisdiction. If you anticipate that your agent will be acting in more than one jurisdiction, you should consider making separate powers of attorney for each jurisdiction.

A jurisdiction is essentially a place that has its own laws. Among others, this can be a county, a state or a country.

If your power of attorney is to be used in a foreign country, you may have to have it "authenticated" or "legalized" before it can lawfully be used. This is a process whereby a government official certifies that the signature of the authority (usually a notary or lawyer) on your document is authentic and, as such, should be accepted in the foreign country. For more information about document authentication and legalization, contact the local consulate/embassy of the foreign country in which you propose your power of attorney to be used.

Most jurisdictions have their own power of attorney forms, but it's generally not mandatory that you use them. For example, lawyers frequently prepare powers of attorney for their clients using their standard terminology rather than adopting state approved forms. As long as the document is headed 'power of attorney', specifies the parties, is signed and dated, and contains recognizable terms normally found in a power of attorney, it should be accepted by most authorities and organizations as such.

In addition to law firms, banks and brokerage houses often have their own power of attorney forms, too. If you want to ensure that your agent can transact business on your behalf with these institutions, you should consider preparing two (or more) powers of attorney — one being your own form and the others being those required by the institutions with which you propose to do business through your agent. You should obviously check with the relevant institutions in advance, to ascertain their specific requirements, and even obtain copies of the forms they prefer to use. That way, you can fill in and sign their form at the same time as you prepare and execute your 'general purpose' power of attorney.

In terms of signing and witnessing, different jurisdictions tend to have different requirements for powers of attorney. These requirements can vary depending on the powers to be conferred on the agent and the type of power of attorney you are executing. As such, you will need to check the laws applicable in your state to see how your power of attorney should be executed. In most cases, however, executing your power of attorney in front of a witness or a notary will suffice.

Witness to a Power of Attorney

To satisfy various jurisdictional requirements, it is advisable that you not use one of the following people as your witnesses:

- your spouse;

- your partner;

- your child;

- your agent or alternate agent;

- the spouse of your agent or alternate agent; or

- employees of a medical facility in which you are a patient.

Your witnesses must be of legal age in your jurisdiction (see Chapter 2 above). They must also have legal capacity and be of sound mind.

Commencement of a Power of Attorney

A power of attorney will start on a date specified in the document or, in some states, upon the occurrence of a specified event. If there is no specified date or event, a power of attorney starts immediately upon notification to the agent, following its execution by the principal and appropriate witnessing.

A durable power of attorney can be drafted to start at either the time of its signing, or upon the incapacity of the principal.

Revocation of a Power of Attorney

Provided you are not incapacitated, you can revoke a power of attorney at any time by sending a 'notice of revocation of a power of attorney' to your agent. This is a written legal notice signed by or on behalf of a person who granted a power of attorney stating that he or she is terminating the powers conferred on the agent under an earlier power of attorney.

There are a number of reasons, practical and personal, why someone might want to revoke a power of attorney. These may be that:

- the power of attorney is no longer necessary as you are now able to act on your own behalf;

- you no longer trust the agent who is acting on your behalf;

- you have found a more suitable person to act as your agent;

- it is no longer practical to have your agent acting on your behalf; and

- the purpose behind originally granting the power of attorney has been fulfilled and you no longer need an agent to act on your behalf.

The revocation of a power of attorney is not effective against the agent or any third party who may rely on it until such time that notice of the revocation has been received by that party. As such, it is common practice to have a written notice evidencing the revocation rather than simply trying to revoke the authority orally. This written document can, in turn, be sent (by recorded delivery, if necessary) to all third parties who may rely on the power of attorney to put them on notice that your agent's authority has been revoked.

Important Points & Recommendation

While a power of attorney can be an exceptionally handy tool, it is important to remember that it is a serious legal document with far-reaching consequences. Therefore drawing up and signing a power of attorney is something that you should not do without due care and forethought. And while you can pick up a power of attorney form online or at a business supply store and then fill it out yourself, you should be cautious about the forms you use. Indeed you should only use forms from reputable vendors such as Enodare. If you are in any doubt as to the adequacy of the forms or what they do, speak to a lawyer before using them.

Resource

For further information on powers of attorney, see our book entitled "Make Your Own Medical & Financial Power of Attorney". See page 267.

CHAPTER 7:
ADVANCE MEDICAL DIRECTIVES

Chapter 7

Chapter Overview

In this chapter, we review advance medical directives as well as the considerations and procedures involved in making them.

CHAPTER 7

ADVANCE MEDICAL DIRECTIVES

What Is an Advance Medical Directive?

An advance medical directive (or an "AMD" as it is also called) is a written statement in which you set out the medical care that you wish to receive during any period in which you are unable to make decisions on your own behalf. You can use AMDs to set out your preferences in relation to the receipt and non-receipt of various types of medical treatments and procedures including life sustaining procedures. These preferences will ordinarily be honored by medical personnel if you are admitted to a hospital or healthcare facility; assuming of course they have a copy of your directive.

Why Do I Need an Advance Medical Directive?

If the absence of having an AMD, state laws will generally allow your close family members to make medical decisions for you during any period in which you are incapacitated and unable to make decisions on your own behalf. While this can of course be beneficial for you, there is always a risk that your family members will make decisions based on what they believe is best for you rather than what you would have actually wanted in the circumstances. More importantly, there is the added risk that the person making these decisions for you might not be someone that you would have entrusted this responsibility to had you the choice. It was in anticipation of these very issues that AMDs were developed. Thankfully, all states now have provisions that allow for the use of AMDs so that people can exercise some control over the medical treatment they receive during periods of incapacity. The most common types of AMD currently in use include a living will and a durable power of attorney for healthcare. We'll discuss each of these in turn below.

Living Wills and Their Background

A living will is a legal document that allows you to express your preferences regarding the receipt or non-receipt of certain life-prolonging medical procedures in the event that you become terminally ill or permanently unconscious and unable to communicate your own wishes. Apart from allowing you to specify your preferences in this respect, it also allows you to designate an agent who has authority to either enforce or revoke the terms of your AMD should the agent feel that the circumstances warrant.

The development of living wills can be viewed as a legal response to advancements made in the medical field over the last 100 years. During that period, both medicine and medical techniques advanced to a point where physicians can sustain life even in the most dire of situations including situations that were once fatal. Physicians can treat diabetes, cancer and even organ failures. In many cases, patients can lead a relatively normal life following the treatment. However, in other cases, the quality of life of the patient is severely affected. In some instances, physicians can keep the body alive but are unable to restore movement or brain activity and the patient is left in a permanent vegetative state. The ability to keep a person alive in such a condition has invariably led to conflicts between the families of the patients and the physicians providing medical care to the patient. Notwithstanding that families may wish to have their loved ones pass away where there is no reasonable prospect of the patient surviving, medical practitioners will wish to exercise a moral and professional obligation to keep the patient alive. Given this clear conflict on interest, it may surprise you to learn that living wills have only been legal for a relatively short period.

In fact, the concept of facilitating a dying person's rights to control decisions about their own medical care was only first raised by attorney Luis Kutner in 1967 and taken up the following year by Florida legislator Dr Walter Sackett. All initial attempts to pass bills to enable people to have this right failed. It was not until 1974, when State Senator Barry Keene presented similar bills in California, that things started to change. Although Senator Keene's initial attempts also failed the bill was finally passed in 1976 with California becoming the first state to legally sanction a form of living will. Other states soon followed and by the next year, living will legislation had been introduced in 43 states and adopted in seven. Within 15 years all 50 states (plus the District of Columbia) passed some form of advance medical directive or living will legislation.

In 1990 the United States Supreme Court became involved when it agreed to hear its first case on the right to refuse or terminate life-sustaining treatment. The case in question was *Cruzan vs. Director, Missouri Department of Health*. On the night of January 11, 1983 Nancy Cruzan rolled her car, and was found face down in bushes neither breathing nor with any detectable heartbeat. Paramedics restored both functions, but she remained unconscious. At the hospital, surgeons implanted a feeding and hydration tube, but all efforts at rehabilitation proved unavailing as Nancy — though able to breathe — fell deeper into a persistent vegetative state.

For six years Nancy Cruzan's physical and mental state grew steadily worse. It became clear that Nancy had no chance of regaining her faculties, and her parents asked the hospital to turn off her artificial nutrition and hydration processes. All agreed that this would cause her death, and the hospital declined to do so without court approval.

The Missouri Supreme Court, affirming a decision of the state court, ruled that a competent person had the constitutionally protected right to refuse medical treatment, even life sustaining treatment. However, it noted the same right did not apply to persons who were in a state of incompetence as they could not legally refuse the medical treatment. As a result, the focus in the Cruzan case changed to considering whether a surrogate could make such a decision on Nancy's behalf.

Missouri had designed its legislation to include surrogates, subject to the procedural safeguard that there was 'clear and convincing evidence' that the patient, while competent, had expressed the desire not to be kept alive in a permanently vegetative state. On appeal, the United States Supreme Court while recognizing a patient's right to refuse life-sustaining treatment through the use of a written document that complies with applicable state law found that this safeguard was both permissible and constitutional where evidence of intention had been documented. However, it ruled that this standard of proof had not been satisfied in the *Cruzan* case. In reaching this conclusion, the court affirmed the state court's decision against the petitioning parents that their case (that Nancy had expressed a strong desire that her life never be artificially maintained) had not been proved.

Fortunately, the Cruzan family did not stop, and were finally able to muster enough proof of Nancy's desire not be artificially kept alive. They eventually won a court order to discontinue her life support, and she finally died 11 days later on December 26, 1990.

Congress has now passed legislation to publicize and support the state laws. These laws go under the name Advance Medical Directives and, rather than actually creating any new forms of directives, they simply validate state laws that create AMDs. The AMD laws derive from the federal Patient Self-Determination Act, 1991 ("PSDA"), passed a short while after the Cruzan decision. The PSDA requires that adult patients admitted to medical care facilities in receipt of federal funding be apprised of their rights to prepare advance healthcare directives which, if prepared, are then entered on their medical records.

How Living Wills Work

In understanding how living wills work in practice, it's important that you realize that living wills only come into effect when:

(i)   you are suffering from a terminal condition, a persistent comatose condition or in a permanent vegetative state;

(ii)   there is no real prospect of your recovery; and

(iii)   you are unable to make and communicate your own healthcare decisions.

It is only at this point will the person nominated under your living will have any ability to enforce or revoke any of the instructions that you have set out in your living will. However, before this person can lawfully act, the law in the majority of states and indeed the terms of most living wills require that two physicians must first personally examine you and agree that you satisfy the conditions referred to above and that the application of medical procedures would only prolong the dying process. If both doctors agree that this is the case, then the medical procedures may be withdrawn or applied, depending on the choices expressed in your living will.

What Is a Terminal Condition?

A terminal condition is an incurable condition caused by disease, illness or injury with the consequence that there is no reasonable prospect that the patient's condition will improve and the expected result is death. Such diagnoses are often common with progressive diseases such as cancer or advanced heart disease.

Did You Know?

A terminal condition is referred to in some states as a terminal illness, a terminal injury or an incurable or irreversible illness.

Often, a patient is considered to be terminally ill when the life expectancy is estimated to be six months or less, under the assumption that the disease will run its normal course. In many cases, where people are correctly diagnosed as being terminally ill, they will cease to be able to properly communicate towards the final stages of their illness. It is in these very situations that living wills can be most beneficial.

What Is a Persistent Comatose Condition?

A persistent comatose condition can generally be described as a profound or deep state of unconsciousness where there is no reasonable prospect of regaining consciousness. In other words, while we are in fact alive, we are effectively asleep and unable to respond to life around us. This condition, which is often caused by accidents or traumas, is similar to a coma save that with a coma there is often an expectation that the patient will regain consciousness at some time in the future.

What Is a Persistent Vegetative Condition?

A persistent vegetative state, which sometimes follows a coma, is a condition which results in a person losing all cognitive neurological function and awareness of the environment around them. However, despite this neurological illness, the individual retains non-cognitive functions and a disrupted sleep-wake cycle.

What Life Support Choices Do I Have Within My Living Will?

There are, generally speaking, three different choices you can make in regards to life-sustaining measures:

- **Option 1** – You can require doctors do everything in their power to keep you alive.

- **Option 2** – You can provide that the only life-sustaining measures you desire to have are artificial tube feeding for nutrition (food) and hydration (water).

- **Option 3** - You can have all artificial life-sustaining treatment withheld, including nutrition and hydration.

Of course, you can to a degree mix some of the above options. However, no matter which of these three options you choose, you will generally always be provided with all necessary pain medication and comfort medication. In addition to the provision of treatment for pain and comfort there are a number of different treatments available to help keep you alive including surgery, respiratory support, dialysis, antibiotics, cardiac resuscitation, blood transfusions, tissue and organ donation and receipt of nutrition and hydration.

Should I Make a Living Will?

Whether or not you decide to make a living will is completely up to you. In making that decision, you will need to consider situations that might leave you in a persistent state of unconsciousness or indeed cause your death. Understandably, these are situations you might prefer not to think about. However, with high-tech medicine adding weeks, months and sometimes years to our lives (rather than often adding "life" to our years) we all run the risk of being incapacitated before we die. This leaves some serious questions for you, and indeed everyone, to ponder and to plan for.

Consider what you would want to happen if a serious accident or illness left you in a situation where:-

- you were unable to speak, move, feel or, worse still, you were in constant pain;

- only a respirator and feeding tube were keeping you alive; and

- your quality of life was virtually non-existent and there was no real hope of improvement.

Would you want to stretch your life out on life support or would you rather let nature take its course? Where would you want to draw the line? When should it end?

Unfortunately, far too many people actually find themselves, without warning and without the benefit of asking those questions, in those or similar situations. These people have no control over the medical care they are receiving. These people have no choice but to "live". You can avoid this if you are practical. Consider your alternatives and make a choice.

If this choice is hard for you to contemplate, think of how it will be for your loved ones if you do nothing. If anything should ever happen to you, they will be the ones who will have to bear the emotional trauma of dealing with your permanent incapacity. They will be the ones that will have to visit you in hospital and make the tough decisions for you. They will be the ones who have to consider how to foot the bill for years of hospital care notwithstanding that there might be no possible chance of recovery for you! They may even end up paying these bills themselves!

We don't mean in this chapter to scare you or to convince you that it's right or wrong to make a living will. We are here to prompt you to think —not to tell you what to think or what you should or should not do or think — just to prompt you into thinking about this very important matter for yourself.

Having the right to deicide what medical treatment you receive, if any, during a terminal illness is what living wills are all about. They allow you to decide these things now, while you can. It is about doing it calmly and without any pressure, and then articulating your wishes in a legal document that will be there to guide your doctors, friends and family if and when you come into the emergency room unable to tell them what you really want. The decision to make a living will is, of course, yours to make!

 Important Note

A living will does not allow you to appoint another to make life-sustaining decisions for you; that power can only be granted under a power of attorney. Your agent under a living will typically only has powers of enforcement or revocation only.

State Requirements for Life Sustaining Medical Treatment

Although you may have a living will, certain states have legal restrictions and requirements concerning medical treatment that must be adhered to notwithstanding the terms of your living will. For example, some states require that you receive medical treatment for a certain period of time regardless of your living will. In these states, if you are diagnosed to be in a state of permanent unconsciousness, laws may require that you receive medical treatment for 60 or 90 days before the doctors can make a decision to implement your wishes as stated in your living will. Or if your condition shows zero brain activity, laws may require that you receive medical treatment for a certain number of hours before the terms of your living will can be implemented.

Other legal limitations may also arise. For instance, the provisions in your state may prevent a living will from being implemented if a woman is pregnant, and may declare that the living will is ineffective during the course of the pregnancy.

To be certain of the effectiveness and legality of your living will, and learn what provisos state law may apply, it's best to contact a lawyer in your particular state — or ask a relevant government agency for information. Alternatively, check out our book entitled *"Make Your Own Living Will"*. To give you a flavor of some of the restrictions that apply, we have set out a brief summary of same below.

State	Overview of State Requirements for AMDs
Alabama	Two witnesses required for an AMD. An AMD will not be valid if the patient is pregnant.
Alaska	No witnesses required for a living will. Two witnesses are required for a healthcare power of attorney.
Arizona	A witness and a notary are required for both a living will and a healthcare power of attorney.
Arkansas	Two witnesses required for both a living will and a healthcare power of attorney. Neither will be valid if the patient is pregnant.
California	Two witnesses required for both an AMD and a healthcare power of attorney. A healthcare power of attorney can also be witnessed by a notary.
Colorado	Two witnesses required for an AMD. A healthcare power of attorney does not require any witnesses.
Connecticut	Two witnesses required for both an AMD and a healthcare power of attorney. The signatures must be notarized. Neither will be valid if the patient is pregnant.

State	Overview of State Requirements for AMDs
Delaware	Two witnesses required for both a living will and a healthcare power of attorney.
District of Columbia	Two witnesses required for both a living will and a healthcare power of attorney.
Florida	Two witnesses required for both a living will and a healthcare power of attorney.
Georgia	Two witnesses required for both a living will and a healthcare power of attorney. A living will is not valid if the patient is pregnant.
Hawaii	Two witnesses required for both a living will and a healthcare power of attorney. The healthcare power of attorney must be notarized. A living will is not valid if the patient is pregnant.
Idaho	Two witnesses required for both a living will and a healthcare power of attorney. A notary can also witness a healthcare power of attorney. A living will is not valid if the patient is pregnant.
Illinois	Two witnesses required for a living will. A living will is not valid if the patient is pregnant. One witness required for a healthcare power of attorney.
Indiana	Two witnesses required for a living will. A living will is not valid if the patient is pregnant. A notary is required for a healthcare power of attorney.
Iowa	Two witnesses and a notary required for both a living will and a healthcare power of attorney. A living will is not valid if the patient is pregnant.
Kansas	Two witnesses or a notary are required for a living will.

State	Overview of State Requirements for AMDs
Kentucky	Two witnesses or a notary required for a living will. A living will is not valid if the patient is pregnant.
Louisiana	Two witnesses required for both a living will and a healthcare power of attorney.
Maine	Two witnesses required for both a living will and a healthcare power of attorney.
Maryland	Two witnesses required for both a living will and a healthcare power of attorney.
Massachusetts	No provision for a format of living will. Two witnesses required for both a living will and a healthcare power of attorney.
Michigan	No provision for a format of living will. Two witnesses required for both a living will and a healthcare power of attorney.
Minnesota	Two witnesses and a notary required for both a living will and a healthcare power of attorney. A living will is not valid if the patient is pregnant.
Mississippi	Two witnesses required for an advanced healthcare directive (includes both a living will and a healthcare power of attorney in the one document).
Missouri	Two witnesses required for both a living will and a healthcare power of attorney. A notary can also witness a healthcare power of attorney. A living will is not valid if the patient is pregnant.
Montana	Two witnesses required for a living will.

State	Overview of State Requirements for AMDs
Nebraska	Two witnesses and a notary required to witness a living will.
Nevada	Two witnesses required for both a living will and a healthcare power of attorney. A notary can also witness a healthcare power of attorney.
New Hampshire	Two witnesses or a notary required to witness both a living will and a healthcare power of attorney.
New Jersey	Two witnesses or a notary or a lawyer is required to witness both living wills and healthcare powers of attorney.
New Mexico	No witnesses required for either a living will or a healthcare power of attorney.
New York	Two witnesses required for both a living will and a healthcare power of attorney.
North Carolina	Two witnesses required for both a living will and a healthcare power of attorney. A living will is not valid if the patient is pregnant.
North Dakota	Two witnesses required for both a living will and a healthcare power of attorney. A living will is not valid if the patient is pregnant.
Ohio	Two witnesses or a notary required for both a living will and a healthcare power of attorney. A living will is generally not valid if the patient is pregnant.
Oklahoma	Two witnesses required for both a living will and a healthcare power of attorney. A living will is not valid if the patient is pregnant.

State	Overview of State Requirements for AMDs
Oregon	Two witnesses required for both a living will and a healthcare power of attorney.
Pennsylvania	Two witnesses required for a living will (includes a healthcare power of attorney in the same document). A living will is not valid if the patient is pregnant.
Rhode Island	Two witnesses or a notary required for both a living will and a healthcare power of attorney. A living will is generally not valid if the patient is pregnant.
South Carolina	Two witnesses or a notary required for both a living will and a healthcare power of attorney. A living will also requires a notary to act as a witness.
South Dakota	Two witnesses required for both a living will and a healthcare power of attorney. A healthcare power of attorney can also be witnessed by a notary. A living will is generally not valid if the patient is pregnant.
Tennessee	Two witnesses required for both a living will and a healthcare power of attorney. A healthcare power of attorney can also be witnessed by a notary.
Texas	Two witnesses required for both a living will and a healthcare power of attorney. A living will is generally not valid if the patient is pregnant.
Utah	Two witnesses required for a living will. A living will is generally not valid if the patient is pregnant. A notary is required for a healthcare power of attorney.
Vermont	Two witnesses required for both a living will and a healthcare power of attorney.

State	Overview of State Requirements for AMDs
Virginia	An advance medical directive requires two witnesses.
Washington	Two witnesses required for a living will. A living will is generally not valid if the patient is pregnant. No witnesses are required for a healthcare power of attorney.
West Virginia	Two witnesses and a notary required for both a living will and a healthcare power of attorney.
Wisconsin	Two witnesses and a notary required for both a living will and a healthcare power of attorney. A living will is not valid if the patient is pregnant.
Wyoming	Two witnesses are required for both a living will and a healthcare power of attorney. A notary is also required for a healthcare power of attorney. A living will is not valid if the patient is pregnant.

Witness Requirements

In order to ensure that a living will is the voluntary act of the person making it, and that this person has not been unduly influenced by their medical condition or by other persons, certain states have limitations on when a living will can be made and who can serve as witnesses.

In several states, you cannot make a living will while you are in the hospital or in a nursing home. It must be made before you go to the hospital (or at least, after you have been discharged, and before you're readmitted with your 'final illness'). In other instances specific conditions will apply before you can make a living will in hospitals. For example, under Georgia law, if you wish to make a living will while you are a patient in a hospital or resident in a nursing home, you will need to have an additional person to witness you signing your living will form.

In the case of a hospital, this third witness must be the chief of the hospital staff or a physician not participating in your care. In the case of a nursing home, it must be the nursing home's medical director or a staff physician not participating in your care.

In most cases, you will need two witnesses to witness the signing of your living will. However, you should be aware that a number of states prohibit certain people from acting as a witness to the signing of a living will. In fact, some of the state forms expressly specify who cannot act as a witness. You should be sure to check the laws of your state to determine who can and cannot act as a witness to your living will. In general, however, the following people are precluded from acting as witnesses in most states: your spouse, children grandchildren, parents, grandparents, siblings, or any lineal ancestors or descendants. Also included are spouses of any of these people. Other persons who should not be witnesses of course would include a person who is named in your last will or who would benefit from your estate (if you died intestate), someone who is a beneficiary of a life insurance policy on your life and finally a person who is directly responsible for your medical care (including employees, agents and patients of any hospital or nursing home that you might be in). The rationale here is that each of those people may potentially gain upon your death and may make decisions based on self-motivation.

You should also avoid using minors or anyone named as an agent in your healthcare power of attorney.

Appointing an Agent to Revoke or Enforce Your Living Will

As already mentioned, some states allow you to name an agent who may either revoke or enforce your living will. It is generally considered that when you name an agent, you are giving that person the power and authority to go to court on your behalf and ask a judge to either revoke or enforce the terms of your living will. However, in some cases, depending on the content of your living will, the agent does not need to go to court, but can merely instruct the medical care providers to either disregard or to enforce your wishes as set out in the living will. Alternatively, the agent may only be able to temporally suspend the operation of your living will so that it is not used at a specific time, but may be used later.

Important Note

Even if you don't appoint an agent under your living will, healthcare facilities and physicians are still obliged to follow the provisions set out in your living will.

Appointing a person to enforce or revoke your healthcare decisions can be useful because it allows for advocacy on your behalf which could help get over difficulties in interpreting your living will. It's also worth remembering that if a physician refuses to respect the terms of your living will you have the right to be transferred to another physician or hospital that will honor the document. An agent can be very useful in ensuring that this happens.

Finalizing Your Living Will

Once you have decided to make a living will, you should check the specific laws that may apply in your state. Many states have specific forms, and in a few states, required language that should be included in your living will. When you have determined the specific laws that apply in your state and what form you need to use, there are a few final steps you should take to ensure that your wishes will be respected when the time comes. Specifically, you should

- discuss the terms of your advance directive with your doctor before you sign it. Make sure you are both comfortable with what it says. He or she may suggest something you hadn't thought of that you might decide to include;

- comply with your state's signature and witness requirements. As mentioned above, states have various requirements about who can be a witness, how many witnesses are needed, and if the directive must be

notarized; and

- provide copies of the signed directive to (1) your doctor and hospital; (2) your agent if one is named; (3) family members; (4) your lawyer and (5) other significant people in your life.

Important Note

Out-Of-State Directives

People often wonder whether advance directives made in one state will be honored in other states. The good news is that the laws of many states provide for the recognition of living wills made in other states. However, there are some states where the law is simply not clear on the issue. While there is a degree of ambiguity in these states, the practical reality is that most healthcare providers will try to abide by your wishes irrespective of whether you use an out-of-state form or not.

In situations where you spend much of your time between a few different states, it might be useful to make a living will in each state just to cover off the possibility that a healthcare provider refuses to recognize an out-of-state living will. It might even be practical to have different healthcare agents in each such state but this is something that you will have to consider carefully.

Terminating Advance Directives

As long as you remain mentally competent and able to manage your own affairs, you may terminate a living will that you have previously made at any time. Incidentally, the same applies to a healthcare power of attorney.

While your advance directive can be revoked orally, even as in some cases it can be made orally, we do not recommend doing so. It's simply too prone to challenge, and too difficult to prove. Rather we would recommend one of the following options:

- physically destroying the living will by burning, tearing or shredding it;

- revoking the authority granted to an agent under a living will by giving notice of revocation in writing; or

- if you have appointed a proxy or attorney-in-fact with power to do so, this person can revoke your directive.

Ordinarily, revocation only takes effect when the revocation is communicated to the agent or the person who may reply on the living will. So if you revoke your living will, you should send copies of the notice of revocation to each person or facility that holds a copy of your living will. This should ensure that the notice is brought to their attention.

Not all states require that your revocation be signed in front of witnesses, but a handful of states do. Even if your state does not require witnesses, it is a good idea to have them sign your revocation. With witnesses, you minimize the chances that your revocation will be challenged or considered ineffective if you move.

Family Discussions

In reality, if you become incapacitated, it will be up to your family to decide whether or not they wish to support the end-of-life decisions that you have made in your living will or whether they will try and fight it with a view to keeping you alive or allowing you to die naturally. It is for this very reason that we recommend that you discuss your personal choices with close family members. At the very least, it will afford you an opportunity to bring them around to your way of thinking. Alternatively, it will open the door for a discussion that may provide you with useful feedback or may even present you with alternatives that you had not considered.

In having this discussion, you should explain to your family members the decisions you have made and why you have made them. It may even be useful to refer to some of the high profile cases in this area such as the *Cruzan* case above or the more recent, substantively similar Terri Schiavo case. In discussing the issue, it's important that you also try and get them to accept the person that you have nominated as your agent under your living will. Otherwise, in addition to the emotional trauma, your family could find themselves amidst a grave conflict should you become incapacitated. It follows that it is also very important that you discuss your wishes with your agent and ensure that he or she is fully aware of what you want to happen should you ever become permanently incapacitated. If you get both your family and agent in line with your thinking on the subject, matters should hopefully run smoothly as between them when the time requires.

Making Your Wishes Known - Legal Vaults™ Wallet Cards

When you have made your advance medical directive, it is a good idea to carry a card in your wallet or purse confirming that you have done so. This way, should you be admitted to a medical facility and unable to communicate, healthcare providers will be alerted to the fact that you have set out your requirements in relation to end-of-life treatments and will be legally bound to honor your wishes. By including on your card the contact names and numbers of key family members, details of your doctor and details of the location of your advance directives if you have any, your healthcare providers will be able to determine your healthcare wishes when most needed.

Resource

For more information on obtaining wallet cards and storing your advance directives electronically so that physicians and medical personnel can easily access them in a time of emergency we recommend visiting the Legal Vaults™ website at www.legalvaults.com.

Healthcare Power of Attorney

As you will have no doubt gathered from the foregoing, the principal limitation of living wills is that they only come into play when you are either terminally ill, or permanently unconscious, and cannot tell your doctors what you want done. It therefore does not apply where, for example, you are unconscious due to a minor accident or illness or where you are suffering from a mental illness. This is where a healthcare power of attorney ("HCPOA") comes into play.

A HCPOA (sometimes called a durable power of attorney for healthcare or a healthcare proxy) is a document that appoints someone of your choice to be your authorized agent (or attorney-in-fact or proxy) for the purpose of making healthcare decisions on your behalf when you are unable to do so yourself. You can give your agent as much or as little authority as you wish to make some or all healthcare decisions for you. And in most states, you can include the same kind of instructions that you would put in a living will and require that your agent abides by them in carrying out his duties.

The authority is effective only when your attending physician or physicians (depending on state law and the terms of your HCPOA) determines that you have lost the capacity to make informed healthcare decisions for yourself. As long as you still have this capacity, you retain the right to make all medical and other healthcare decisions.

In your healthcare power of attorney, you may also limit the healthcare decisions that your agent will have the authority to make. The authority of the agent to make healthcare decisions for you generally will include the authority to:

- give informed consent,

- refuse to give informed consent, or

- withdraw informed consent

to any care, treatment, service, or procedure designed to maintain, diagnose, or treat a physical or mental condition.

Choosing a Healthcare Agent

The person you choose to be your healthcare agent (also called an "attorney-in-fact" or "proxy for healthcare decisions") should be a trusted individual who is also knowledgeable and comfortable discussing healthcare issues. Because this person may need to argue your case with doctors or family members, or even go to court, an assertive yet diplomatic individual may be the best individual to represent your interests. Your representative should be well aware of the choices you have made in your advance directives and should support those instructions.

For most, the person chosen to act as an agent is a spouse, partner or close family relative. However, while you of course trust these people you will need to consider whether they have the resolve to make the tough decisions that you have asked them to make when the time comes. If you are in any doubt, you may wish to chose an alternative agent or appoint a second agent who independently has full authority to carry out your instructions. However, we would not ordinarily recommend the appointment of joint agents as it can lead to arguments and conflicts between them which result in delays in important medical decisions being made.

In choosing an agent, you should consider the person's age, emotional ability, how well they know you, their views on your wishes and the right to life generally, their religious beliefs, whether they have any financial or other interest in your survival or death and the availability of that person generally to act as your agent.

In certain states, a spouse can lose the right to act as an agent for his or her spouse if the couple are legally separated or divorced unless you provide otherwise in your HCPOA.

Similar to the position with living wills above, your agent or healthcare proxy should not be someone attending to your healthcare as there is a danger of a conflict of interest arising in such circumstances as it is in the healthcare provider's financial interest to keep treating you rather than curing you!

Important Note

As a practical matter, it's useful to appoint the same person as your agent under both your living will and healthcare power of attorney – of course, the choice is up to you in this respect!

Alternate Healthcare Agent

When making your advance directive, it's always a good idea to appoint one or more alternate agents. An alternate agent is someone who will perform the duties of the first named agent should they be unable or unwilling to do so (for whatever reason). If the alternate agent is required to act, he or she will be bound by the same duties and responsibilities as the original agent.

Do I Need a Healthcare Power of Attorney and a Living Will?

Most estate planners agree that the best approach in dealing with healthcare issues is to have both a living will and a HCPOA. As already pointed out, using a living will in isolation is problematic as it only relates to end-of-life decisions. As such, in order to cover all other medical decisions, it always advised to make a HCPOA to supplement it. It's even better when you can combine both into one document as it lessens the likelihood of any conflict arising where there are two separate documents. In fact, many states allow you to combine the two documents.

Conclusion

You now have two important ways to prepare for the possibility that you may sometime be unable to decide for yourself what medical treatment to accept or refuse. You should consider the use of a living will and a healthcare power of attorney carefully as they form an integral part of estate planning.

 Resource

For more information on living wills and to make one of your own, see our book entitled "Make Your Own Living Will". See page 266.

CHAPTER 8:

PROBATE AVOIDANCE MEASURES

Chapter Overview

In this chapter, we'll look briefly at some of the problems with probate and introduce you to ways in which you can avoid it!

Chapter 8

CHAPTER 8

PROBATE AVOIDANCE MEASURES

Probate Avoidance

As discussed in Chapter 5, probate is a court supervised administrative process by which the assets of a deceased person are gathered; applied to pay debts, taxes, and expenses of administration; and then distributed to the beneficiaries named in the deceased's last will and testament. Where there is no will, the assets go through a similar process known as intestate administration. For ease, we will refer only to the probate process in this chapter.

While some states have procedures to allow for a speedy probate process for 'small estates', the average probate takes at least six months to complete. Of course, if there are any difficulties in locating beneficiaries or assets, or if there are legal challenges to the validity of the deceased's will, this time frame can increase dramatically and probate can take several years to complete. Only when the process is completed in full should the executor transfer the remainder of the deceased's estate to the relevant beneficiaries.

The probate process can be expensive – particularly if it drags on. The cost of probate differs from state to state and is generally determined by either state law or custom and practice in a particular area. When all the costs associated with probate are added up, the resulting cost is often between 1% and 7% (or even more) of the value of the deceased's probatable estate. As some of these probate costs are set by state law there is very little that you can do to mitigate or reduce them - other than utilize one or more of the known probate avoidance measures discussed in this chapter!

There are a number of legal mechanisms which you can use to avoid probate including:-

- pay on death, transfer on death or joint accounts;

- transfer on death securities;

- insurance policies;

- joint ownership of property;

- revocable living trusts;

- lifetime gifts; and

- having property valued at or less than the limit allowed for a simplified procedure that many states allow when estates are small.

These particular methods have a number of advantages. For example, they are flexible and easy to set up. Bank accounts and insurance policies can be established, amended and terminated with little hassle or cost. As a result, you can easily and quickly change the beneficiaries of your assets or the amount by which you intend them to benefit by means of a simple visit to your local bank or insurance broker. And after you pass away, the only document that your beneficiaries will typically need to present to the bank or insurance company in order to receive the proceeds of their inheritance is a death certificate evidencing your death. With that, the financial institution should be happy to make arrangements to have the relevant proceeds transferred in to your beneficiary's name or paid out to them.

There are however also disadvantages to using these methods. You need to be very careful to ensure that all of your probate alternatives are working together to avoid probate and, more importantly, to distribute your assets in accordance with the overall objectives of your estate plan. You will need to pay specific attention to the beneficiaries named in joint bank accounts, insurance policies, the manner in which real estate is held etc. Any lack of attention could result in one person receiving a lot more than you had intended to the detriment of someone else. And, don't forget, by the time the problem materializes you may not be around to remedy it!

Pay on Death or Transfer on Death Accounts

One of easiest ways to avoid probate is by having a pay on death (POD) or transfer on death (TOD) account. The majority of states now have laws that allow account holders to designate a named beneficiary who will receive the proceeds of their bank and/or investment accounts after they have died. When the account holder dies, the money in the designated account goes directly to the named beneficiary without going through probate.

Generally, there is no need to open a new account in order to avail of the advantages of a pay on death account. In many cases, you can simply add a 'POD designation' to an existing account by simply adding the name or names of the beneficiaries to that account. The relevant financial institution will be able to give you information on what exactly needs to be done in order to add the designation.

During the account holder's lifetime the designated beneficiaries have no rights whatsoever in relation to the account or its proceeds; and the account holder can close the account or remove the POD designation at any time. It is only after the death of the account holder that the beneficiaries become entitled to the proceeds.

TOD accounts are similar to POD accounts but are more commonly used to transfer ownership of stocks, bonds and mutual funds.

Transfer on Death Securities

The Transfer on Death Security Registration Act provides for the transfer on death of stocks, shares, bonds and other financial instruments and securities. Similar to the TOD and POD accounts referred to above, these securities can be transferred on death to named beneficiaries free of the requirement to pass through probate.

To date, the following states have adopted the legislation:-

State	Status	Effective Date
Alabama	*PASSED*	May 29, 1997
Alaska	*PASSED*	Jan 1, 1997
Arizona	*PASSED*	Jan 1, 1996
Arkansas	*PASSED*	Aug 13, 1993
California	*PASSED*	Jan 1, 1999
Colorado	*PASSED*	Jul 1, 1990
Connecticut	*PASSED*	May 14, 1997
Delaware	*PASSED*	Jun 26, 1996
District of Columbia	*PASSED*	Apr 27, 2001
Florida	*PASSED*	Jan 1, 1995
Georgia	*PASSED*	Jul 1, 1999
Hawaii	*PASSED*	Apr 29, 1998
Idaho	*PASSED*	Jul 1, 1996
Illinois	*PASSED*	Jan 1, 1995
Indiana	*PASSED*	Jul 1, 1997
Iowa	*PASSED*	May 26, 1997
Kansas	*PASSED*	Jul 1, 1994
Kentucky	*PASSED*	Aug 1, 1998
Louisiana	-	-
Maine	*PASSED*	Mar 27, 1998

State	Status	Effective Date
Maryland	*PASSED*	Oct 1, 1994
Massachusetts	*PASSED*	Nov 5, 1998
Michigan	*PASSED*	Dec 20, 1996
Minnesota	*PASSED*	Jun 1, 1992
Mississippi	*PASSED*	Mar 24, 1997
Missouri	PASSED	Jan 1, 1990
Montana	*PASSED*	Oct 1, 1993
Nebraska	*PASSED*	Sep 9, 1993
Nevada	*PASSED*	Jun 1, 1997
New Hampshire	*PASSED*	Jun 18, 1997
New Jersey	*PASSED*	Sep 20, 1995
New Mexico	*PASSED*	Jul 1, 1992
New York	*PASSED*	Jan 1, 2006
North Carolina	*PASSED*	Oct 1, 2005
North Dakota	*PASSED*	Jul 1, 1991
Ohio	*PASSED*	Oct 1, 1993
Oklahoma	*PASSED*	Sep 1, 1994
Oregon	*PASSED*	Sep 29, 1991
Pennsylvania	*PASSED*	Dec 18, 1996
Rhode Island	*PASSED*	Jul 9, 1998

State	Status	Effective Date
South Carolina	*PASSED*	Jun 13, 1997
South Dakota	*PASSED*	Jul 1, 1996
Tennessee	*PASSED*	Jul 1, 1995
Texas	-	-
Utah	*PASSED*	May 1, 1995
Vermont	*PASSED*	Jul 1, 1999

Retirement Accounts

Similar to POD accounts, its also possible to designate beneficiaries of retirement accounts such as IRAs and 401(k)s. Your broker or financial advisor should be able to assist with the designation should you so wish.

Remember that you need to designate the beneficiary on the account documents not in a will, living trust or elsewhere. If you do not comply with the relevant requirements, the proceeds may well end up going through probate.

Joint Accounts

Another easy way to avoid probate is by having joint accounts. Where an account is held in the name of two or more persons and is designated with the right of survivorship, then when one of the account holders die, the surviving account holders will automatically acquire the deceased account holder's interest in the account. Whoever is the last surviving joint owner will ultimately own the proceeds of the account outright.

Where a transfer occurs on survivorship, there is no need for probate. The surviving account holder(s) will simply need to provide a copy of the deceased account holder's death certificate to the bank and the bank can then remove that person's name from the account.

Custodial Accounts

People often decide to set aside funds in the form of bank accounts, certificates of deposit or similar securities as a nest egg for their minor children, grandchildren or others, to cover things like college expenses or simply to give them a start in life. One of the most common ways of doing this is by means of a custodial account.

A custodial account is similar to a trust in many ways but is not actually a trust. With a custodial account, the proceeds or assets (where the account is an investment account) are placed under the control of a person known as a custodian. The custodian will have no beneficial interest in the account and will simply manage the account on behalf of the minor beneficiary until he or she reaches a specified age.

It's important to note that once the custodial account is set up and the beneficiary named, the proceeds of the account then beneficially belong to the beneficiary. As such, you can't take it back. Moreover, if the account generates any income that income also typically belongs to the beneficiary (there are some exceptions to this where the account is used to avoid tax) and tax returns may need to be made.

The account will automatically terminate when the beneficiary reaches a specified age. Almost all states have a maximum prescribed age under either the Uniform Gifts to Minors Act (UGMA) 1956 or the Uniform Transfers to Minors Act (UTMA) 1986. For details of the age applicable in your state, see Chapter 2.

Turning back to probate, custodial accounts will not form part of your probatable estate because the gift is deemed to have been made when the account was set up not when you die or when the custodial account terminates.

Savings Bonds

Saving bonds, like bank accounts, can be held jointly and, like POD accounts, can contain a pay on death designation. In the case of jointly held savings bonds, these will pass to the survivor(s) on the death of the other bond holder(s). Also, where there is a POD designation, the bonds will pass to the named beneficiary on your death. In each case, probate will not be needed.

If the bonds are not held jointly or there is no POD designation, the bonds can only be redeemed by the executor. However, they may be reissued to the beneficiary under a will upon a request from the executor accompanied by a copy of the death certificate and the executor's grant of representation. Of course, this will be done as part of the probate process.

Life Insurance Proceeds

A life policy is another example of a simple means by which you can avoid probate. Where you designate a named beneficiary under your life insurance policy, the proceeds of the policy which are payable on your death will pass directly to the named beneficiary without the need to go through probate. However, if your estate is named as the main beneficiary (which is unusual) or if no beneficiaries have been named or if the named beneficiaries have died, the proceeds will need to pass through probate.

The insurance proceeds payable on your death are considered to be part of your estate for federal estate tax purposes and are ordinarily taxable. However, this can be avoided by transferring ownership of the policy to another person while you are still alive!

Joint Ownership of Property

Whether or not the property that you own at the time of your death will need to be probated depends on how the title to that property is held. Typically, property can be held in three different ways:-

(a)   joint tenancy (survivorship);

(b)   tenancy by the entireties; and

(c)   tenancy in common.

Joint Tenancy

We've already touched on the concept of joint tenancy in relation to bank accounts. The same principle applies to real estate. Where a property is held under a joint tenancy, each of the property owners has an undivided percentage interest in the entire property. To illustrate this, an example is often useful. So let's, for example, take a case where four people own a property equally under a joint tenancy arrangement. Each of the four owners has an entitlement to a 25% interest in the entire or whole of the property. However, because each owner has an entitlement to a percentage of the whole, rather than having a divided and defined 25% interest in the property, he is entitled to access and take actions in respect of the entire property and not simply 25% of it.

As mentioned above, where the surviving joint tenant dies, their share passes to the remaining joint tenants. Taking our example again, where one of the four property owners die, their share passes to each of the other three survivors automatically and each of the survivors then becomes entitled to an approximate 33.33% (or 1/3) interest in the property.

The key point to take from the above is that the share passes from the deceased joint owner to the remaining joint owners without the need for probate. It follows that probate can either be reduced or even eliminated by converting solely owned assets into jointly owned assets – held under a joint tenancy. This type of ownership permits the jointly owned assets to simply pass directly to the surviving joint owners on the death of one of the owners – no need for probate.

Tenancy By the Entireties

A special type of joint tenancy known as a 'tenancy by the entirety' is recognized between married couples in some states. Under this form of joint ownership, if a married couple owns property as tenants by the entirety, then each spouse must obtain the consent of the other before dealing with the property in any way that would affect the rights of the other. This includes putting in place a mortgage over the property. Each spouse lacks the power to freely dispose of their interest under their will, or in any other way, as the principle of survivorship applies between the spouses.

Important Note

States that recognize a 'tenancy by the entirety' include: Alaska*, Arkansas, Delaware, District of Columbia, Florida, Hawaii, Illinois*, Indiana*, Kentucky*, Maryland, Massachusetts, Michigan*, Mississippi, Missouri, New Jersey, New York*, North Carolina*, Ohio, Oklahoma, Oregon, Pennsylvania, Rhode Island, Tennessee, Utah, Vermont, Virginia and Wyoming.

*States that allow tenancy by entirety for real estate only

Tenancy in Common

A tenancy in common is one of the most common forms of property ownership in most states. A tenancy in common is created where two or more people purchase a property together as 'tenants in common'. As tenants in common, each of the parties own a separate and distinguishable part of the property. To take the example of our 4 property owners above, if the arrangement was a tenancy in common, each of them would own 25% of the property in their own right and would be free to sell that 25% to any person at any time and/or to dispose of their interest under their will. The right of survivorship does not apply here.

Community Property

Community property states have different rules governing probate, so it's important to understand your own state's rules when planning the distribution of your estate on your death.

At the date of writing there are nine community property states namely Arizona, California, Idaho, Louisiana, Nevada, New Mexico, Texas, Washington and Wisconsin. In Alaska couples can opt to have their property treated as community property under the terms of a written property agreement.

Each of the above states has special laws that dictate how married people can own and dispose of their property – both real and personal.

Important Note

Real property is property such as land, buildings and real estate generally. Personal property can broadly be defined as including all other property which a person can own.

In a community property state, the law broadly provides that all earnings generated during the course of a marriage and all property purchased during the marriage is considered *community property* and therefore equally owned by each spouse. Therefore if, for example, one spouse earns $100,000 per year as an executive, while the other earns $40,000 as a freelance writer, then each spouse shall be deemed to "own" $70,000 of those earnings. In addition to salary, property purchased by one spouse in his or her own name with money he or she earned during the marriage will also be regarded as community property. Similarly, debts incurred by either spouse during their marriage are regarded as debts of the couple rather than individual debts.

Separate property, on the other hand, includes property received by a spouse during their marriage by means of a gift or bequest under a will. It also includes any property owned by a spouse before they got married which that spouse has kept segregated from community property during the marriage. Similar to the position regarding debts above, all debts incurred by spouses prior to marriage are considered separate debts of each spouse.

Separate property can also include anything that one spouse gives up in favor of the other spouse in writing.

The distinction between community property and separate property becomes important when determining which of a spouse's assets can be freely disposed of under the terms of their will. In community property states, on the death of a spouse, half of the community property owned by the couple will go to the surviving spouse, unless the deceased spouse's will directs otherwise (i.e. provides for the transfer of part or all of their share of the community property to the surviving spouse). Otherwise, the surviving spouse is free to dispose of their share of community property as well as their separate property as they desire.

Revocable Living Trust

An additional way to avoid probate is to establish and fund a revocable living trust. This type of trust is established by writing a trust agreement. In essence, under the terms of the trust agreement, the creator of the trust (known as a grantor) will transfer ownership of certain of his assets into the trust. The trustee of the trust (which is also actually the grantor) will hold and manage the assets on behalf of the trust. The trustee can manage, invest, and spend the trust property as he or she sees fit for the benefit of the grantor and for the benefit of the ultimate beneficiaries of the trust.

Because the grantor will not own any property in his or her individual name after the assets have been transferred into the name of the trust, the assets won't need to be probated. When the grantor dies, the person nominated as the 'successor trustee' under the terms of the trust agreement will step into the grantor's shoes and will distribute the proceeds of the trust to the named beneficiaries in accordance with the terms of the trust agreement.

We will discuss revocable living trusts in greater detail in the next chapter.

Gifts During Your Lifetime

Giving away property while alive helps avoid probate since anything that one doesn't own when they die, does not go through probate!

Probate Free Transfers of Assets

If the deceased owned boats or motor vehicles and their total value does not exceed a specified amount (usually between $25,000 to $75,000 – varying from state to state) ownership of these vehicles can be transferred probate free in most states to a surviving spouse/partner or other next of kin.

Additionally, any salary, wages, accumulated vacation and sick benefits, plus any other fringe benefits, may according to the laws of certain states be paid to the surviving spouse/partner, adult children or next of kin without the need for probate.

Simplified Transfer Procedures for "Small Estates"

Generally speaking, if the deceased did not have any property to transfer, probate would not be necessary. However, the deceased's relatives may nonetheless decide to conduct probate proceedings if there are debts or taxes owed. This is done for the purpose of ensuring a proper wind up of the deceased's estate. If a decision is made to probate an estate for these specific reasons, it would be advisable to speak to an attorney to ascertain the best options available to you.

Generally speaking however, where a person holds property, it will, as a general rule, be the size of their estate in monetary terms that will determine whether probate is required. Most states have adopted streamlined and simplified probate procedures for what is called the transfer of 'small estates', with the limitation currently ranging from estates with net values of as low as $500 to as high as $140,000. If the deceased's estate is under the permitted limit set out above, a simple certification procedure can be used instead of normal probate thereby avoiding a lengthy and costly probate administration procedure.

However, in reality, as most people generally have a home or land valued over the above amounts, few people are able to avail of this exemption from the probate process.

CHAPTER 9:
REVOCABLE LIVING TRUSTS

Chapter Overview

In this chapter we review revocable living trusts: what they are, their benefits, how to set them up and maintain them over a lifetime. Revocable living trusts are a popular probate avoidance method and therefore a very useful and important tool in estate planning.

Chapter 9

CHAPTER 9

REVOCABLE LIVING TRUSTS

What Are Living Trusts?

A revocable living trust is a particular type of 'inter vivos' trust (meaning a trust made between living people) that is used for estate planning purposes. It is a written agreement created for the simple purpose of holding ownership of assets outside of your probatable estate during your lifetime, and then distributing these assets to named beneficiaries after your death.

Specifically, with a living trust, you as the creator of the trust (known as the "grantor") transfer property from your personal ownership to a trust that you have created. You then name yourself as the initial trustee of that trust. The result is that while legal ownership of the trust property changes from you to the trust, you (as initial trustee) continue to maintain control over your property and can continue to enjoy it in same way as you did prior to transferring it to the trust. When you die, a person appointed by you and known as a successor trustee (which is a little like an executor) steps in, takes control of the trust and transfers the trust assets to the people named as beneficiaries under the trust agreement.

Living trusts can be stated to be revocable, meaning that you as the grantor reserve the right to revoke or terminate the trust and resume personal ownership of the trust property at any time. In addition, you maintain discretionary rights to add to or withdraw assets from the trust property, to change the terms of the trust, and even to make it irrevocable at some time in the future.

Important Note

Not everyone needs a living trust. As a general rule of thumb, you might conclude that you do not need a living trust where you are young and healthy, you can more easily transfer your assets (or some of them) by other probate avoidance methods or where you do not own any (or very little) property of value. So consider your own situation carefully before making any decision to create a living trust.

Advantages of Living Trusts

There are a number of advantages to using living trusts. These include the following:-

1. **Avoids probate**

   The main advantage of a living trust is that by transferring assets out of your name and into that of the trust, the assets will no longer be deemed to be part of your estate. As such, when you die, there is no need to have these assets go through the probate process before they can be transferred to your beneficiaries. This allows for a quick distribution of your assets by your successor trustee to the beneficiaries named in your trust agreement.

2. **Saves money**

   By avoiding probate, you will also save your heirs a substantial amount of money in filing fees, costs, attorney fees and executor fees.

3. **Avoids publicity**

   With probate, your will (together with a schedule of all your assets) is filed in the probate registry and becomes a public document open for inspection by anyone upon payment of a small fee. By contrast, a living trust is essentially a private contract entered into between you (as grantor) and you (as trustee) and, as there is no public filing requirement, details of your assets and the beneficiaries of same can remain confidential.

4. **Provides protection during incapacity**

A growing number of older people are transferring their assets into living trusts because they want to avoid them being placed under the management of a court-appointed guardian if they become unable to manage their affairs. With a properly drafted living trust, if you become disabled or otherwise unable to manage your estate, your living trust avoids the need for a court-mandated conservatorship by nominating a person known as a successor trustee (similar to a guardian) to manage the trust assets during any period of incapacity.

5. **Very difficult to contest**

One of the often overlooked benefits of a living trust is that its privacy makes it much more difficult to contest by comparison to a will. As the contents of a living trust are not publicly known, unlike wills which are available to the public for inspection, attorneys are less likely to spend their own time and money pursuing a lawsuit with unknown probabilities of success.

6. **Management of children's inheritance**

If you are concerned about the future welfare of your children, should you die before they reach an age where they can take care of property themselves, you can set up one, or more, separate child sub-trusts within your living trust, for the benefit of each child. The terms of the sub-trust will ordinarily provide that the child will not inherit the property from the sub-trust until he or she reaches a specified age of your choosing. Until the child or children, as the case may be, reach the designated age, the successor trustee will manage the trust property on their behalf in accordance with the terms of the living trust.

You can also appoint a custodian under the Uniform Transfer to Minors Act to hold and manage assets on behalf of a child beneficiary until that beneficiary reaches an age specified by you in the trust agreement, which will be between 18 and 25 years depending on your state's law.

7.   Flexible

Living trusts are extremely flexible. You can change the terms of the trust, add and withdraw assets, change the beneficiaries of those assets, change the successor trustee or even terminate the trust at any time.

Disadvantages of Living Trusts

There are a number of disadvantages to using living trusts. These include the following:-

1.   Failure to fund the living trust

One of the biggest problems associated with living trusts is the failure to properly transfer assets into the trust itself. This act of transferring assets is commonly referred to as 'funding the trust'. Where the assets are not properly transferred to the trust, they remain part of your probate estate and are not subject to the terms of your trust. If you have not provided for the transfer of these assets under your will, which is likely, they may end up being unintentionally gifted to the person entitled to the residue of your estate under your will or, where there is no will, to a relative on intestacy.

If any of the assets you propose transferring to your trust have forms of 'title documents' associated with them, you must ensure that the title is properly transferred from your personal name into the name of the trust.

2. **Doesn't completely avoid delays in distribution of assets**

One of the principal reasons for delays in the probate process is caused by the necessity to resolve complicated tax issues before distributing assets to the beneficiaries of the deceased person's estate. An executor of your estate will not be inclined to carry out all of your required distributions under your will until he knows the full extent of your tax liability. This unfortunately can take up to eighteen months in some instances to determine and resolve. More unfortunate however is the fact that the same problem exists equally in relation to a living trust as a person is taxed as if the living trust doesn't exist. In other words, for tax purposes you will be deemed to own the assets in the living trust personally, while for probate purposes you will not.

Another common problem stems from the collection of assets, in particular life insurance proceeds. It can take months to obtain these proceeds, and again the problem exists both for an executor appointed under a will and a successor trustee appointed under a living trust.

So, while a living trust is not going to eliminate delays caused by tax issues or the collection of certain assets, it can speed up the distribution process in respect of other assets due to the lack of court intervention over the acts of the successor trustee. This should therefore go some way towards quickening the distribution process!

3. **Lack of court supervision**

One of the benefits of the probate system is that the court often watches over the distribution of your estate and, in doing so, protects the interests of your beneficiaries. However, no such supervision occurs with a living trust as the responsibility for effecting and overseeing the distribution of your trust assets rests solely with your designated successor trustee. This can be disadvantageous in circumstances.

4. **Limited financial savings for smaller estates**

The real determination as to whether a living trust will save you money depends on how much probate fees would have been paid had the trust assets gone through probate rather than passing through your living trust. If the estate has a small monitory value, you may find that the probate fees payable in your state are quite low having regard to the costs of establishing and maintaining a living trust.

5.   **No protection from creditors**

Depending on state law, a revocable living trust will not ordinarily protect the trust assets from your creditors. In the same way as trusts are transparent for tax reasons, your creditors have a right to go after those assets as if they were still legally in your name.

There are some exceptions to the general principle above. The placing of assets into an <u>irrevocable</u> living trust before you incurred the debt in question can sometimes prohibit a creditor from suing the trust. However, the problem with irrevocable living trusts is that you cannot get the assets back yourself either! The same principle applies when you die. As a revocable living trust becomes irrevocable when you die, protection may or may not be afforded to the assets that are contained within it – depending on the state in question and the circumstances surrounding the placing of assets in the trust in the first instance.

One of the principal drawbacks from not going through the probate process is that no time limit is imposed on creditors within which they can take claims against your estate. With probate, all creditors must notify the executor of any claim they have within a specified time limit. If they fail to notify the executor on time, their claim becomes statute barred and they cannot recover against the estate or your trust. The opposite is the case with living trusts. No time limit is imposed on your creditors and, as such, they can take claims against you or your will after you have died. Moreover, even when the trust is wound up and the assets distributed to the beneficiaries of the trust, they have the right in many states to sue the beneficiaries for the debts you owed – up to the maximum of the benefit they received.

For the above reason, it's often quite useful to have some asset go through the probate process in order to restrict the rights of creditors to take action against your estate and your trust.

The Role of the Initial Trustee

When it comes to living trusts, you will usually appoint yourself as the initial trustee of the trust. Where there are two grantors, such as in the case of a shared or joint trust (discussed in detail below), both grantors are usually appointed as co-trustees. Allowing grantors to serve as the initial trustees is a key feature of revocable living trusts as the whole purpose behind a living trust is to bypass probate in a manner which allows you the right to retain complete freedom to deal with and control your assets.

You may of course decide either at the outset or at a later date that you would prefer to nominate someone else to act as trustee of the trust. That is perfectly fine as the trustee will be obliged to act in accordance with your instructions as grantor of the trust – provided of course the instructions are legal! However, if someone else is acting as trustee of your trust, they will need to obtain an identification number from the Internal Revenue Service (IRS) for the trust and thereafter make income tax returns on behalf of the trust. We recommend that you see a lawyer if you choose not to act as trustee of your own trust. The removal of day-to-day control over your assets could have significant legal and practical consequences.

However, from a practical perspective, given that you were able to manage your assets and affairs while the assets were in your name, there is no reason why you cannot manage them as trustee. The reality is that as trustee of your own revocable trust you don't really owe any duties to anyone apart from yourself. As such, you can simply carry on managing your affairs as you always have provided you don't breach the terms of the trust.

It is important to note that you do not need to file any special tax returns on behalf of the trust. You simply report any income the trust property generates with your own income tax return in the same way that you always did (or, at least, should have!).

Appointing a Co-Trustee

You may decide, for whatever reason, that rather than hand over the management of your trust assets to another person entirely, you would simply like to engage someone to assist in the management of your trust property. You can do this quite easily by appointing someone as a co-trustee of your trust. As co-trustees, both of you would have authority to act on the trust's behalf. Again, while there is no real difficulty with having someone else act as trustee of your trust or even have someone act as a co-trustee, we recommend that you speak to a lawyer before you do this as the terms of your trust document may need to be tailored to cater for this eventuality.

Successor Trustees

Your successor trustee is the person who assumes control of the trust after you, as initial trustee, become incapacitated and/or die. In the case of a shared or joint trust, your successor trustee will take over control of the trust when both trustees are incapacitated or dead. A successor trustee has no authority to act while any of the grantors remain alive or capable of managing the trust. Your trust deed will identify the person or persons who will act as successor trustee(s) of your trust. In most cases, this is usually a relative or a family friend.

It is important to note that even though you name someone in the trust agreement to act as successor trustee, he or she is under absolutely no obligation to carry out the role and cannot be forced to do so. It is open to anyone named as the successor trustee to decline to act. Where this happens, the next named successor trustee will take over the management and administration of the trust. If no alternate is named or none of the named alternates are willing to serve, the beneficiaries of the trust will need to petition the local court to appoint someone to fill the role unless they have authority under the trust agreement to appoint a replacement successor trustee.

One of the most important aspects of your living trust is your choice of successor trustee(s). Do not choose a trustee just because they are a family member or close friend — choose someone that you trust implicitly; someone that you know is competent and capable of handling the demands of a successor trustee's role. You also need to choose someone who is honestly willing to do the job for you. There isn't much point in having to almost force someone into doing it. They need to be happy and ready to accept the task, and if they are not, they are most likely not the candidate for the job.

The Role of the Successor Trustee

A successor trustee takes control under two circumstances – one on the incapacity of the grantor, and the other on the death of the grantor. We will look at each in turn.

Role of Successor Trustee During the Incapacity of the Grantor

The first thing your successor trustee will need to do will be to locate the living trust agreement. Normally, a living trust agreement will contain a clear set of instructions for determining whether or not the grantor is incapacitated or not. More often than not, the terms of the trust will require one or sometimes two doctors (which we recommend) to certify that the grantor is unable to comprehend or to competently manage their affairs. Once the doctors certify incapacitation, the successor trustee stands in and takes control of the trust property.

Next, your successor trustee must ensure that you are in receipt of appropriate medical attention. Usually, the terms of a living trust will allow for the successor trustee to apply an element of the trust assets towards your care and welfare. If you have no insurance or assets outside the trust to fund that medical care, it's important that the successor trustee acts with the utmost haste.

If you have any children or dependents, your successor trustee will also need to arrange for their care. There should be specific instructions in the living trust to deal with such matters. Also, if you have any assets, your successor trustee will need to manage them so that their value is preserved. Finally, your successor trustee will need to obtain a taxpayer identification number and file annual income tax returns for your revocable trust.

Hopefully, you will recover from your incapacity. If you do, everything goes back to normal as the successor trustee no longer needs to act on your behalf!

Role of Successor Trustee Following the Death of the Grantor

When you, the grantor, pass away, it becomes your successor trustee's responsibility to assume control of the trust estate and administer it in accordance with the terms of the living trust agreement. The administration process involves the collection of assets, payment of debts and taxes and the distribution of assets to the ultimate beneficiaries of the living trust. In the majority of cases these beneficiaries will be your partner, spouse and/or children; however you, as the grantor, have the right to pass your trust assets to virtually anyone. Of course, spouses have certain rights so if you are married your freedom will be restricted.

In any event, let's take a brief look at what's generally involved in the 'administration' process.

1. **Obtain certified copies of the death certificate**

   One of your successor trustee's first tasks following your death will be to procure copies of your death certificate. The certificate, together with an Affidavit of Trust, should be presented to third parties (courts, banks, financial institutions, insurance companies, etc.) in order to establish that the successor trustee is lawfully entitled to deal with the trust assets.

   A death certificate can generally be obtained from the State Office of Vital Records or from the Department of Health, but there are some variations from state to state. The successor trustee could also contact your general practitioner or funeral director each of whom should be able to procure a copy of your death certificate.

2. **Obtain tax identification number for trust**

   Next, your successor trustee will need to make an application to the IRS in order to obtain a tax identification number for the trust. The application can be made using the IRS Form 1041 (http://www.irs.gov/pub/irs-pdf/f1-41.pdf)

3. Collection and management of trust assets

Having obtained a death certificate and made an Affidavit of Trust (which will be required when dealing with the trust assets), the next task for your successor trustee is to take possession of the trust's assets and to evaluate what debts, claims, taxes, and other expenses will be payable by the trust. Your successor trustee should work very closely with the executor of your estate in order to determine what assets have been transferred into the trust.

Important Note

An Affidavit of Trust is a declaration sworn by you in front of a notary public confirming that you are the trustee of the trust and attaching relevant pages of the trust (but not all of them) to evidence your appointment as trustee. You will require this when dealing with banks and other financial institutions. Your successor trustee will also need to make a similar affidavit in due course.

Your successor trustee should commence the process by reviewing the trust agreement and trust records in order to establish what assets have been transferred into the trust and what debts might exist. It is important that your successor trustee actually secures the assets. Securities (especially bearer bonds), title deeds, jewelry, and other items of substantial value should be physically located and placed in a safe deposit box or safe. Other assets should be insured against risks such as fire, damage, theft, loss and liability, as appropriate. Once the assets are secured, the successor trustee should proceed to obtain a valuation of all assets as well as an assessment of any liabilities incurred by the trust.

Your successor trustee should:-

- **Claim life insurance proceeds**

  Your successor trustee should contact any insurance company

with whom the grantor held a policy of life insurance. If the living trust was named as a designated beneficiary on that policy your successor should made a claim for any insurance proceeds due to the trust.

- **Gain access to bank accounts and other financial accounts**

  Each financial institution that held an account for the trust should be notified of your death so as to commence the process of releasing control of the proceeds of the accounts to the successor trustee and/or the trust beneficiary.

- **Identify debts owed by the grantor**

  As noted, your successor trustee should ensure that any valid debts against the trust are discharged from the trust assets.

- **Maintain proper accountings of trust assets**

  Your trustee will have a duty to prepare an annual accounting in respect of the trust assets (unless the beneficiaries waive their rights to such an accounting). The accounting should display the assets held by the trust at the date of your death as well as current market valuations. The accounting should also include any income received, any expenditure made and any assets added to or taken out of the trust. In order to prepare this, the successor trustee will need to keep meticulous records of all disbursements from the trust.

4. Preparing and filing tax returns

The successor trustee and the executor of your estate are collectively responsible for the payment of the various taxes set out below.

- **Federal estate tax**

As trusts are transparent for tax purposes, the extent of your assets, both inside and outside the trust, will need to be appraised following your death. If the value of your assets exceeds the estate tax threshold ($1 million for 2012) then estate tax will become payable at the rate of 35% (2012) on the excess. It is the responsibility of your successor trustee *and* your exccutor to determine if estate tax is due and, if so, to make the appropriate tax return.

- **Income taxes**

  A final income tax return will need to be made for the final year of your life. The return should be made on IRS Form 1040. Again, the payment of tax should be coordinated with the executor.

- **Trust income tax returns**

  Following your death, all income generated by your trust will need to be accounted for to the IRS. The return for the trust will be made on IRS Form 1041 for each calendar year. It is the sole responsibility of the successor trustee to ensure that these returns are made. If your living trust is a shared trust (described below) two separate tax returns will need to be made after your death.

- **State taxes and pick-up taxes**

  Finally, your successor trustee and executor will also need to discharge any state taxes or pick-up taxes that may be owed by your estate.

6. **Transferring property to beneficiaries**

Once all of the assets have been collected in and all debts and taxes paid or provided for, the successor trustee can distribute the remaining trust assets in accordance with the terms of the living trust. The assets will either be distributed in cash or in kind if the trust includes specific tangible assets.

Of course, in order to properly carry out the distribution, the beneficiaries will need to have the trust assets re-registered in their names by the successor trustee. The successor trustee will need to go through the process for transferring title in the trust assets over to the beneficiaries. After the re-registration, the assets are deemed effectively transferred to the beneficiaries of the trust. In each case, the successor trustee should have each beneficiary sign an acknowledgement to confirm that he or she has received the distribution in question.

7. **Administering a child's trust**

The duties of the successor normally terminates once he has distributed the trust assets to the beneficiaries of the trust. However, where the grantor has created a sub-trust for any of his children or indeed any other child in the living trust, the successor trustee will need to continue acting as trustee if he has been named trustee of the child's trust. In essence, he will need to manage the trust assets left to the child until such time as the child, or children if there is more than one, reaches the age specified in the trust agreement. This will greatly add to the task of the successor trustee as he or she will need to ensure that the trust assets are properly invested and secured for the period of the child's trust as well as make provision from time for the welfare, upkeep and education of the child. Only when the last child reaches the age specified in the trust document can the successor trustee formally distribute the remaining assets and wind down the living trust. This may well be years or even decades after the grantor has passed away.

8. **Winding down the trust**

The length of time that it takes to settle the trust and distribute assets is often dependent on whether an estate tax return is due. If a return will be due, then it is typically prudent to wait until after a closing letter is received from the IRS to make final distributions. This can take up to 18 months, or more if the estate is audited, after the date of death to receive. However, if no estate tax is due, the trust can usually be wrapped up in a number of months; assuming of course that there are no on-going trusts established under the terms of the living trust itself!

Fiduciary Duties of the Successor Trustee

While it is not the purpose of this book to provide a comprehensive list of a successor trustee's duties, it is useful for you to have an understanding of their role and duties so that you can decide who is best for the role. As with the executor of your estate, the successor trustee of your living trust owes you a fiduciary duty.

Some specific fiduciary duties include the duty to:

- adhere to the terms of the trust;

- act personally in the management and administration of the trust;

- act in the best interests of the beneficiaries of the trust;

- supply annual reports as well as information regarding the trust and its assets to the beneficiaries;

- invest prudently;

- keep trust assets separate from those of the successor trustee; and

- carry out the role of trustee without payment – unless the terms of the trust provide otherwise or the trustee is a professional trustee.

Changing Trustees

While you are alive, you can amend the trust agreement to change the proposed trustee at any time. However, in order to deal with the changing of trustees after your death, specific provisions will need to be inserted into your trust deed. For example, where a successor trustee wishes to resign you should include provisions to ensure an orderly transition from the resigning trustee to the successor trustee. In this regard, you could require that the resignation of a trustee will not become effective until at least fourteen to thirty days after written notice of the resignation has been given to you, if living, or to the current trust beneficiaries of the trust, if you are not living. These notice requirements will ensure that you or the trust beneficiaries of the trust have sufficient time to have a successor trustee in place before the resigning trustee actually resigns.

If a beneficiary of your trust, on the other hand, is either unhappy or concerned about the manner in which a successor trustee is dealing with the trust property, and the situation cannot be resolved by discussion between them, he or she will have the option of petitioning the court to effect the removal of the successor trustee. However, in the absence of having just cause, the beneficiary will find it extremely difficult to remove the successor trustee.

The Beneficiaries of Your Living Trust

The beneficiaries to a trust are almost identical to those of a will. Therefore we will only briefly review the generalities of living trust beneficiaries. For full detailed information on beneficiaries please refer to Chapter 2 or to our separate dedicated book, *"Make Your Own Living Trust & Avoid Probate"*

Let's have a brief look at of the types of beneficiaries you can have:

- **Primary Beneficiaries** are those whom you name to receive specific property. These beneficiaries include individuals, institutions and groups.

- **Alternate Beneficiaries** are the ones you name to get property left initially to a primary beneficiary who has predeceased you or refused the gift

- **Residuary beneficiaries** are those who will receive all the property of the trust not left to either primary or alternate beneficiaries.

Should you wish to change beneficiaries, it is a fairly simple matter to amend the trust and add or remove names. If you wish, you can also name specific alternate beneficiaries for each and every gift made to a primary beneficiary. The alternate beneficiary will take the gift if the primary beneficiary predeceases you or refuses to accept the gift.

If you wish, you can include a *"no-contest clause"* in your living trust. This is a condition placed in a living trust (or will for that matter) which is used to discourage beneficiaries from trying to claim more than you have left them. Under a "no-contest clause" a beneficiary who challenges the terms of your living trust (most likely because he or she wants more that you have left them!) loses all his or her inheritance under that document.

Types of Living Trust

The two main types of living trusts used for estate planning purposes are basic living trusts and AB Trusts. A basic living trust, which can be used by an individual or a couple, has the primary objective of avoiding probate. An AB Trust, on the other hand, goes one step further by saving on estate taxes. We'll discuss each of these types of trust in more detail below.

Living Trust for an Individual

If you're single, you probably want your living trust to transfer your property to your relatives and friends following your death. If this is the case, then the basic living trust could be right for you. As already explained, to create a basic living trust you simply sign a trust agreement between yourself as grantor and yourself as trustee. Under the terms of the trust agreement you will nominate someone to act as your successor trustee and also specify who is to receive the benefit of your trust assets following your death. When you die, your successor trustee steps in and transfers the trust property to the beneficiaries named in your living trust.

If you have any children, you can use your trust to leave property to them; with care of that property being vested in a property guardian or trustee until they reach the age you have specified in your trust agreement.

Important Tip

Remember that in order to appoint a testamentary guardian to care for your minor children following your death, you will need to make that appointment in your will. You cannot do this in your trust.

Living Trusts for Couples

Couples, whether married or not, often own property together. If you are part of a couple, you can decide whether you want to create an individual trust for your own separate property or whether you want to create a joint or shared living trust with your partner.

If you are married, then you will need to consider and take into account whether you are living in a community property state or whether you are living in a common law state. In brief, depending on what state you are living in, the law will determine what amounts to your individual property and what amounts to joint marital property. You can transfer your individual property to a living trust as well as your share of your community property.

There are four principal types of living trust arrangement that couples can create:

- Each spouse or partner prepares their own individual living trust;

- Both of you prepare one shared living trust;

- Both of you prepare a basic AB trust; or

- Both of you prepare an AB disclaimer trust.

We discuss each arrangement in detail below.

- **Individual living trusts**

  For couples, the use of individual trusts can make a lot of sense where you and your spouse/partner own most of your property separately rather than jointly. In such cases, you may want to ensure that your spouse does not gain control over your assets once you transfer them to the trust while at the same time ensuring that your assets are not tied up in probate. An individual trust is ideal in such circumstances.

  However, there are drawbacks to using individual living trusts. For example, in order to transfer a jointly held asset into a trust, it may become necessary to divide title to the asset into two separate deeds and thereafter have each spouse transfer their half of the asset to their trust. This can become expensive and messy and, sometimes in such circumstances, it makes sense to create an additional trust to hold the jointly held assets. For this reason, it is often recommended that couples avoid individual trusts in favor of shared living trusts. Of course the choice is yours!

- **Basic shared living trusts**

  Many couples use one basic shared living trust to avoid probate and to handle both their co-owned property and their separately held property. Here, both partners establish the trust and as such, both act as co-grantors and co-trustees of the trust. As co-grantors, each partner can nominate beneficiaries for their individual or separate property and for their portion of joint property. In addition, each partner can unilaterally call for the return of their assets to them and/or revoke the trust at any time. When the trust is revoked, the assets return to the parties that placed them in the trust. Each partner retains full ownership and control of all their separate property as well as their share of the jointly owned property.

  When one of the partners dies, the trust automatically splits into two separate trusts – we'll call them the 'first trust' and the 'second trust'. The deceased partner's property and share of the joint property is automatically transferred in to the first trust. The terms of the first trust immediately become irrevocable which means the surviving partner cannot amend them in any way. Thereafter, the surviving partner in his/her capacity as successor trustee distributes the property in the first trust in accordance with the deceased partner's wishes as set out in the trust document. In many cases, the deceased partner will leave his or her assets to the surviving partner's trust – the second trust.

All of the remaining trust assts are transferred to the second trust, which continues to exist as a stand-alone trust – similar to an individual trust. This trust is revocable by the surviving partner in the same way as an individual trust. When the surviving partner dies, the trust assets will be distributed in accordance with the terms of the trust in the usual way.

- **Basic AB trusts**

  An AB trust can be useful where the combined value of your estate and that of your spouse is likely to exceed the individual unified tax credit ($1 million in 2012). Federal estate tax law provides that, for the 2012 tax year, no tax will be assessed on a person's estate if the value of their taxable estate, at death, was worth less than $1 million. Where the value of that estate exceeds this amount, the excess is taxed at the rate of 35% (45% in 2009). While estate tax was repealed in its entirety for 2010, in 2011 the estate tax assessment threshold increased to just $1 million.

  Generally, one spouse or partner will leave their entire estate to the other spouse partly to allow the survivor to have the benefit of their assets and partly because the transfer is tax-free. However, if as a result of this transfer, the value of the surviving spouse's estate ultimately ends up exceeding the unified tax credit at the time of his or her death, then estate tax will be payable on the excess. This charge to tax, or rather part of it, can be avoided with proper planning. The use of an AB trust is one such method that can achieve this.

With an AB trust, on the death of one of the spouses, the trust splits into two separate trusts – Trust A and Trust B. Assets equal to the value of the estate tax threshold amount are transferred to the deceased spouse's trust A for the benefit of the beneficiaries - usually his or her children. The remainder of the trust assets is transferred to Trust B. There is however one very significant caveat. The terms of the AB trust provide that the surviving spouse will become a "life beneficiary" of Trust A. As such, the survivor can have the use and benefit of the assets in Trust A for the rest of their life without being given complete ownership of any of it! The surviving spouse can therefore use all of the income generated from the property in Trust A for their own support and upkeep, but they cannot sell the assets or deal with them in any way.

When the surviving spouse dies, all of the trust property in both Trust A and Trust B is distributed to the beneficiaries in accordance with the terms of the AB Trust. As the deceased spouse's share of the trust property was never transferred to the surviving spouse, the deceased spouse is still able to avail of the their estate tax exemption ($1 million in 2012). As such, the deceased spouse's funds in Trust A can be passed on to his or her beneficiaries tax-free. Similarly, the surviving spouse's (who is now dead incidentally) can also pass an amount equal to estate tax threshold to his or her beneficiaries. This, in essence, means that the beneficiaries, who are most likely the children of the couple, can receive a combined amount tax-free – an amount which is far in excess of the amount which they would have received under the terms of a will or an ordinary living trust which contain no tax panning provisions.

Despite the benefits, there are a number of disadvantages associated with the use of AB living trusts including:

- control over the trust property may be restricted – the rights of the surviving spouse are limited to an entitlement to the interest or other income derived from the trust property, use of the trust property, and utilization of the trust property for the purpose of discharging costs incurred in connection with his or her health, education, support and maintenance;

- the spouses may need to pay legal or accounting fees to facilitate the division of property between the Trust A and Trust B;

- tax returns must be filed on behalf of Trust A;

- separate records must be kept regarding the trust property in each of the two trusts; and

- because of the uncertain nature of estate taxes, you cannot be assured of any tax benefit.

- **AB disclaimer trust**

   An AB disclaimer trust works the same as the basic AB trust, apart from one very important factor – the right of the surviving spouse to determine how much, *if any*, property goes into Trust A.

   The AB disclaimer trust is a trust that names the surviving spouse as the beneficiary of the other spouse's estate (which is tax free in the normal course). However, on the death of the first spouse, the surviving spouse has the option of renouncing or disclaiming all or part of the trust assets which he or she is to receive from the deceased spouse if the combined value of their estates exceeds the estate tax exemption threshold amount at the time of the first spouse's death. The disclaimed assets would pass to a credit shelter trust (similar to Trust A for the Basic AB Trust discussed above) for the benefit of the surviving spouse – who will have a life interest in these trust assets. However, if the assets are allowed to pass to the surviving spouse's Trust B, he or she will have full control and 'ownership' over them as if they were in an individual trust.

   Again, and similar to the situation with an ordinary AB trusts, the assets in both Trust A and Trust B will be distributed on the death of the surviving spouse.

Conclusion

You should carefully consider the use of each of the above types of trust before deciding that any of them would suit your particular circumstances.

Remember, as well as the advantages, each comes with its own set of particular disadvantages. You should choose wisely and tailor any living trust to your own, unique circumstances.

Transferring Assets to Your Living Trust

As discussed, there are two primary reasons why you might establish a revocable living trust. Firstly you want you want to provide for the management of your property during any period of incapacity. Secondly, you want to avoid the costs and delays associated with having your assets go through the probate process. Both are perfectly legitimate and solid reasons for establishing your living trust. However, if having established the trust you fail to properly transfer assets to the trust, or fund the trust as the term is called, your efforts will have been in vein. Without complying with the required formalities to transfer assets to your trust, these assets will be deemed to be your personal assets and will end up going through the probate process; or the intestate administration process if you have failed to make a last will and testament.

What Assets Should Be Put in Your Living Trust?

One of the principal goals of any living trust is to avoid the cost associated with probate, with the general rule being that the more an asset is worth, the more it will cost your estate on probate fees. It follows therefore that you should, at the very least, consider transferring your most valuable assets to you living trust. However, it is entirely up to you what you decide to include or leave out.

You are free to include assets such as your home and other real estate, bank and saving accounts, investments, business interests, antiques, jewelry, personal belongings, royalties, patents, copyrights, stocks, bonds and other securities, money market accounts and so on.

In deciding what assets you want to transfer to your living trust, always bear in mind that where you are acting as both the grantor and trustee of your own trust, you always have the right to call for the return of any assets you transfer into the trust.

The reality is that you don't need to put everything into your living trust in order to save money on probate. See the previous chapter for details of the items which do not go through the probate process. There is no need to include these items in your living trust, as they will pass to the designated beneficiaries automatically and outside of the probate net.

Title to Assets Transferred to a Living Trust

While there has been considerable debate as to whether property transferred to a living trust needs to be re-titled in the name of the trust, we recommend that all assets which have any form of title document should be re-titled in the name of the trust. To transfer assets which do not have title documents to your trust, all you typically need to do is simply list them in the schedule of assets contained at the back of your trust agreement.

In order to re-register the title of an asset from your personal name in to the name of your living trust, you simply sign a document transferring the legal title in that asset from you to the trust. The transfer will be between, for example, John Smith and John Smith, trustee of the John Smith Family living trust dated 1 January 2012. Then when it comes to signing the transfer document, you will sign the document in your own right as (for example) "John Smith" AND you will also sign on behalf of the living trust using the words "John Smith, Trustee".

Any failure to properly transfer the asset can result in it remaining as part of your probate estate.

Transferring Property to Your Trust

Given the vast diversity of assets that you can transfer to your living trust, we will take a very brief look below at some of the most commonly transferred assets and how those transfers should be effected so as to ensure that they become part of your trust estate.

Real Estate

In order to transfer real estate into your living trust you will need to prepare a deed of transfer. In most cases this can be pretty straightforward. However, there are certain issues that you need to watch out for as there are many different nuances associated with the transfer of title to real estate – such as the type of deed required, title insurance, mortgages, out-of-state property, homestead rights and tax on transfer deeds. As such, we recommend that you engage the services of an attorney qualified in your state to assist with the transfer of any property located in your state.

 Important Tip

Remember to notify your insurance company when transferring your personal property!

Cars, Boats and Other Vehicles

You can transfer a vehicle to your trust in much the same way as you would transfer it to a third party. You should note that the majority of states have a specific form that can be used for registering the transfer of a vehicle.

Cash Accounts

In order to transfer the title to your current (checking) accounts, savings accounts or money market accounts you can either change the name on the account (from "John Smith" to "John Smith, trustee of John Smith Family living trust"; for example) or close the account and open a new one. Each financial institution can advise on which of the two methods they will allow.

United States Savings Bonds

While U.S. Savings bonds can be transferred into your living trust, you will need to contact your bank to obtain the appropriate form to transfer the bonds as well as details of the procedure involved. Once the transfer is completed, the bonds will be re-issued in the name of your living trust.

Broker Accounts

It is also possible to transfer a broker account held with a brokerage firm or with a mutual fund company to your living trust. Similar to the position with bank accounts, you will need to contact the firm/company to determine whether they can simply change the name on the account or whether they will have to close the existing account and open a new one in the name of the trust.

Publicly Quoted Stocks

There are two ways to transfer stock in a publicly quoted company to your living trust. You can contact the company's share registrar (or transfer agent as it's often called) or you can contact your broker and ask him to open an account in the name of the living trust and have the stock re-issued to the trust.

Retirement Plans

Due to their complexity, tax advantages and unique distribution features pension plans, profit-sharing plans, IRSs, Keoghs, SEPs and other qualified pension plans should never be transferred into a living trust without first consulting your tax advisor.

Other Property

If you want to transfer any other property to your living trust, a simple deed of assignment should suffice. However, if there are specific documents required to effect transfers of property (such as share transfer forms for a corporation) then you should use the required form. If you are uncertain as to how to proceed, we suggest that you contact an attorney.

Finally, remember you can transfer assets out of your living trust and back to you by simply reversing the process outlined above. As grantor and trustee, you ordinarily have full authority and capacity to do this.

Revocation of Your Living Trust

While it is not too common an occurrence, a living trust can be revoked at any time. In order to revoke a living trust, you must do the following:

- in your capacity as grantor, prepare and serve a notice of revocation on the trustee of the trust (which is generally the grantor). The notice will inform that trustee that the trust is terminated and will call for the return of the trust assets to the grantor. Note that in the case of a shared living trust or an AB Trust, notwithstanding that there are normally two co-grantors, either co-grantor alone is legally entitled to terminate the trust by serving a notice of revocation;

- arrange for the transfer of legal title in the trust assets to be transferred from the living trust back to the grantor personally; and

- ensure that any beneficiary designations in favor of the living trust should are amended. In this respect, we are talking about pay-on-death accounts, life insurance, etc.

Pour-Over Wills

A pour-over will is a special type of will that is used in conjunction with a living trust. Instead of providing for the distribution of all of your assets and property, the pour-over will simply provides that any of your property that has not been transferred into your living trust before your death will 'pour-over' into your living trust after you die. In this way, it ensures that these assets will be distributed in accordance with the provisions set out in your living trust.

In essence a pour-over will is like most other wills. It provides for the revocation of other wills, names an executor and appoints a guardian for minor children. The one real difference is that it has one specific beneficiary – your living trust.

While a pour-over will has certain advantages, the major draw back is that the property passing under the will may have to go through probate. This in turn means that the beneficiaries of your living trust have to wait for probate to complete before the assets are transferred to the trust. They will also have to wait for the successor trustee to make the subsequent distribution from the living trust. The chances of a speedy distribution in those circumstances are slim unless the grantor's probatable estate outside the living trust is small enough to avail of the expedited procedures available for the probate of 'small estates'.

Notwithstanding the above, the use of a pour-over will can be beneficial where circumstances exist which deter people from putting all of their property into their living trusts during their lifetimes. For example, due to restrictions imposed by certain states and insurance companies, it can often be difficult to buy, sell, or insure assets held in a living trust.

In other situations, people who have established living trusts simply forget to transfer all of their assets to the trust or don't get an opportunity to do so. For example, someone might have received an inheritance a few days before they pass away and simply never had an opportunity during their last days to make the transfer.

The use of a pour-over will is therefore a good means to avoid intestacy and having state law determine how your assets should be divided. Similarly, there is no reason why you cannot simply have a will of your own with a standard residuary clause similar to that set out in the living trust – it more or less accomplishes the same thing in most instances. However, there may be situations where, under the terms of a living trust, the residuary trust estate is passed to a minor beneficiary and a sub-trust is set up in the living trust to cater for the management of the child's property until he or she is sufficiently old to take control of the property. In such circumstances, it makes sense to flow the excess assets into the living trust rather than providing for a separate trust for the same child under the terms of your will

All in all, it is fair to say that whenever a living trust is used, it can be wise to have a pour-over to cover assets not transferred to the trust.

CHAPTER 10:
ESTATE TAXES

Chapter Overview

Estate tax in the United States is a tax imposed on the transfer of a deceased person's "taxable estate", whether such property is transferred via a will or according to the state laws of intestacy. The following chapter provides some insight into different types of taxes. For an in-depth understanding of estate tax issues, it is advised that you contact an accountant or tax attorney.

Chapter

10

CHAPTER 10

ESTATE TAXES

Estate Taxes

When accountants, lawyers and others who deal with these matters refer to 'estate tax' they are usually referring to federal tax, not state tax. This distinction is made for three main reasons: (i) many states do not impose an inheritance or death tax; (ii) federal tax is likely to devour more of an estate than state tax will; and (iii) reducing the federal estate tax will often result in a reduction of state taxes as well.

Estate Tax Update

Estate tax was temporarily "phased out" by the government during 2010. Until mid-December 2010, there was a degree of uncertainty as to whether estate tax would be reintroduced and, if it was, the precise manner that it would take upon reintroduction. This uncertainty came to an end on 17 December, 2010 when President Obama signed new legislation into law which extended the previous estate tax cuts introduced by the Bush administration. For the two years 2011 and 2012, the estate tax rate has been reduced from 55% to 35% and the estate tax exemption threshold (also called a 'coupon') has been increased to $5,120,000 – up from $3,500,000 in 2009. In addition, the gift tax exemption has increased from $1,000,000 to $5,120,000.

Federal Estate and Gift Tax

The U.S. tax system generally taxes transfers of wealth. This means the federal government usually charges a tax when money or other assets are transferred from one person to another. Keeping this general rule in mind helps to understand estate and gift taxes.

Gift tax, unlike most income taxes, is assessed on the giver, and not the receiver. As such, if you make a gift of cash or an asset to someone, you will be assessed to a gift tax unless you fall within the scope of the exceptions set out under the headings below. When gift tax is payable, you will need to record details of the gift on IRS form 709. Like many other tax forms, the gift tax form is generally due April 15th in the year following the year in which you made the gift.

Similarly, when you die, another transfer of assets takes place from you to someone else. Like the gift tax, the estate tax is imposed on the giver, which in that case will be your estate. A federal estate tax return is reported on IRS form 706, and is due to be filed with the IRS within nine months of the date of your death unless extended.

Everyone's "Coupon"

The gift and estate tax have to be considered together, because they are intertwined in that both are taken into account when calculating the maximum amount that you can give away or, if you die, your estate can transfer without incurring a charge to tax. Simply speaking, the maximum amount you can transfer without incurring gift or estate tax is like a "coupon". When the value of your gifts and estate are calculated, you can apply this "coupon" to minimize or avoid the tax. You will only have to pay gift or estate tax if your gifts and/or transfers exceed this "coupon" amount.

For example, in 2012 the "coupon" for gifts is $5.12 million. That means that you can transfer up to $5.12 million in gifts during your lifetime and there won't be any gift tax due. If the gift is made to someone other than your spouse, it won't matter who received the gift just that the total value of gifts didn't exceed the "coupon". However, if you exceed the value of the "coupon", you'll owe tax on the excess gift(s). Under current law, the rate of gift tax varies based on the year of the gift. A chart detailing the rate of gift and estate tax can be found under the heading "How to Determine the Estate Tax" below.

For example, if you give $2,000,000 of taxable gifts to each of your three children over your lifetime, you'll have made $6,000,000 in taxable gifts. You can use your "coupon" to avoid tax on the first $5,120,000 but you'll owe tax on the other $880,000.

How does this relate to estate taxes? Well, for most years, you also have a "coupon" for estate taxes. However, as the government views every dollar you gave away during your lifetime as a dollar less that can be taxed in your estate when you die, this "coupon" will be reduced by the amount of the gift tax "coupon" that you have used during your lifetime! So, while there is also a "coupon" for estate tax, it is linked to the gift tax "coupon"; and more specifically to the amount of that gift tax "coupon" that you have already used.

Example: Let's say you made those three $2,000,000 gifts to your children, and still had $7 million in your taxable estate when you died in 2012. In 2012, the estate tax "coupon" is $5.12 million, so at first blush we might calculate that your estate owes estate tax on $1,880,000, which is the difference between the $7 million value of your estate and the estate tax "coupon".

However, that calculation would be wrong because the estate tax "coupon" is reduced by any gift tax "coupon" that you have already used. So, because you used the full $5.12 million gift tax "coupon" during your lifetime, your estate tax "coupon" is reduced by $5.12 million to $0! On the other hand, if you had used only $500,000 of your gift tax "coupon", your estate tax "coupon" would be $4,620,000 million ($5,120,000 estate tax "coupon" less $500,000 of gift tax "coupon" used).

Example of Coupon

Margot gave Rick and John a total of $4 million during her lifetime that used up most of her lifetime gifting exemption of $5.12 million. Margot died in 2012. The estate tax threshold in 2012 was $5.12 million. However, in order to determine whether Margot had reached her estate tax exemption threshold, the gifts she made during her lifetime will be taken into account. As such, on her death, her exemption would only be $1.12 million ($5.12 million less the $4 million gift tax exemption used).

What Is the "Coupon" Amount?

As the chart below shows, both the gift tax and estate tax "coupons" are each currently set at $5.12 million having increased substantially over the last few years.

Year of Gift or Death	Gift Tax Coupon	Estate Tax Coupon
2010	$1,000,000	No estate tax
2011	$5,000,000	$5,000,000
2012	$5,120,000	$5,120,000

How to Determine the Estate Tax?

The first question to ask when trying to determine the amount of federal estate tax which might be due by your estate is "What is the fair market value of everything you own, control, or have an interest in at the date of your death?" In answering this question, you will need to include all assets you own such as cash, investments, real estate, and personal property such as cars, boats, art and the like. Estate tax is also levied on the life insurance policies in your name where you have a right of ownership in the policy.

The total value of all of these items is called your "gross estate". Your taxable estate is your gross estate less certain deductions. These deductions may include mortgages on your assets, debts you owe, estate administration expenses, property that passes automatically to your surviving spouse, and bequests to qualified charities (more on the deductions for spouses and charities below). The value of your gross estate minus these deductions is referred to as your "taxable estate".

Once you have calculated your taxable estate, estate tax may be owed if the value of the taxable estate exceeds the unused portion of your estate tax "coupon".

Just as the value of the "coupon" changes depending on the year in which you make a gift or die, the percentage of the tax assessment also changes.

Year of Gift/Death	Maximum Gift Tax	Maximum Estate Tax
2009	45%	45%
2010	35%	N/A
2011 and 2012	35%	35%

State Taxes

Not every state imposes a separate state tax on estates or inheritances. Florida, for instance, imposes no state death tax. Where there is such a tax, it is likely to be one (or a combination) of three types of tax: (1) death tax, (2) inheritance tax, or (3) pick-up tax.

State Death Taxes

Generally, when people use the phrase "death tax", they are referring to state taxes levied on an estate upon death. The amount of state tax due, if any, is determined on a state-by-state basis according to that state's tax laws and is often calculated in a manner similar to federal estate tax.

State Inheritance Taxes

In states with inheritance tax laws, inheritance tax is paid by the person who receives assets either under a will or on intestacy. As with intestacy laws, beneficiaries are divided into different classes based on the closeness or remoteness of their relationship to the deceased. One tax rate may apply to all assets in the estate, or the rate may vary depending upon who receives what property. Generally speaking the closer the person receiving a gift from the deceased is to the deceased (in terms of blood line), the lower the tax rate on the transfer of property to that person. Thus, depending on what class the beneficiary falls into, he or she will be taxed at a specific rate.

Inheritance Tax States			
Indiana	1-20%	Nebraska	1-18%
Iowa	5-15%	New Jersey**	11-16%
Kentucky	4-16%	Pennsylvania	4.5-15%
Maryland **	10%	Tennessee	5.5-9.5%
** Both Inheritance and Estate tax in this state			

State "Pick-Up" Taxes

Some states base all or a portion of their state death tax on the amount of credit that the federal estate tax used to allow for state death taxes. Prior to 2005, federal estate taxes could be reduced by a credit for the amount of state death taxes paid. The result was that the federal estate tax was a "maximum" tax that was paid partly to the state and partly to the federal government. Many states therefore would "pick-up" their tax revenue by pegging their state death taxes at the amount of the federal credit that you could claim for state death taxes. After 2001, the federal government gradually eliminated the credit for state death taxes. However, some states chose to continue to charge a pick-up tax based on what the federal credit was in 2001, even though the federal credit is no longer available.

For all three of the types of tax a state might assess, some states will have a "coupon" equal to the federal tax "coupon", meaning that if there is no federal estate tax there is no state estate tax. However, many states have chosen not to increase their "coupons" at the same rate that the federal law does, so the state "coupon" may be smaller, resulting in state estate tax even where there is no federal estate tax.

Marital Deduction

Remember the gift and estate tax "coupon" for federal taxes? Historically, it was unique to each individual/estate and could not be used by anyone else. That meant that you had a "coupon" and your spouse had a "coupon" and they were non-transferable.

The "coupons" are not used up by gifts made or estates transferred to a spouse who is a U.S. citizen. Instead, federal gift/estate tax applies an unlimited deduction to those transfers. In other words, you can gift or transfer an unlimited amount of property to your U.S. citizen spouse and there is no gift or estate tax on that transfer.

That's the good news. The bad news is that the marital deduction can be, in some instances, just a waiting game whereby the government allow you to transfer your property tax free to your spouse with the view that it could later be taxed when your spouse dies or gives it away. Historically your spouse could not use your gift/estate tax "coupon" prior to the introduction of the Tax Relief, Unemployment Insurance Reauthorization, and Job Creation Act of 2010, in December 2010, he or she had more to transfer to his or her beneficiaries and heirs but without the benefit of an increased the "coupon". However, in December 2010, President Obama signed this legislation into law which entitled a person to use any unused element of his or her deceased spouse's coupon. There is a slight catch to this in that the right could be lost of the surviving spouse remarries. The law is also set to expire on the 31st December, 2012.

Consider this example: Your last will & testament provides for your spouse to inherit everything you own when you die. At your death, your net taxable estate is $6,000,000 and your spouse also has an estate worth $6,000,000. Since your spouse was the recipient of your estate, the unlimited marital deduction applies and there is no estate tax due as a result of your death regardless of the applicable "coupon". If your spouse dies in 2012, under current law your spouse's maximum "coupon" will be $10,240,000 - $5,120,000 of his or her own plus $5,120,000 of yours – assuming neither of you previously used any element of your coupon. Of course, to the extent that either of you used your coupon, this amount will be deducted from the $10,240,000 coupon. Ultimately, your spouse's estate will be subject to tax on the excess of $1,760,000. At a tax rate of 35%, that translates to a tax of $616,000.

Important Note

A surviving spouse may lose the right to use his or her deceased spouse's coupon if he or she remarries!

Non-Citizen Spouses

The unlimited marital deduction is available only when you give or leave your assets to a spouse who is a U.S. citizen at the time the transfer is made. Some types of credit shelter trust planning mechanisms are also only effective if your spouse is a U.S. citizen. If your spouse is not a citizen, your estate plan must include more sophisticated trust planning designed to keep the assets in the United States managed by a U.S. trustee so that the trust can qualify for the marital deduction that is otherwise only available to U.S. citizen spouses. This is called a Qualified Domestic Trust, or QDOT. For more information, speak to your attorney.

Charitable Deductions

You probably already know that you get an income tax deduction when you donate to a charity during your lifetime. You can also save on estate taxes by giving to charity. Any bequest you make from your estate to a qualified charity is exempt from federal estate tax. You can also combine estate tax planning and income tax planning by setting up a trust with a charity as one of the beneficiaries.

Charitable Remainder Trust

The most common charitable trust is a charitable remainder trust, or CRT. With this type of trust, you donate an asset or assets to the trust during your lifetime. You can continue to get some income from the trust assets, but the charity gets the remainder of what's in the trust when you die or when the term of the trust otherwise ends. Because you have made a donation to the trust, you will be allowed to take an income tax deduction equal to the estimated value of the charity's remainder. You have also removed the asset in the trust from your estate, so it won't be subject to estate taxes when you die. Yet you still can enjoy a regular payout from the trust assets. The amount of income you get from the trust may be either a fixed percentage of the assets you donated to the trust or a percentage of the trust's value each year. Of course, if you choose to peg your payment on the value of the trust, your payment will fluctuate as the value of the assets in the trust fluctuates.

Some CRTs are especially attractive if you have assets that have appreciated in value. By placing the asset into the trust, you may be able to minimize the capital gains taxes you would otherwise have had to pay when you sold the asset.

Let's look at how a CRT would work in an example: Norm and Marian own vacant land that they purchased many years ago. The value of the land has gone up considerably, so they would have to pay significant capital gains tax if they sold it. Yet, the land doesn't produce any income for them in their retirement. Rather than sell the land, pay the capital gains tax and then invest the after-tax proceeds to produce income, they decide to create a CRT and donate the land to the trust.

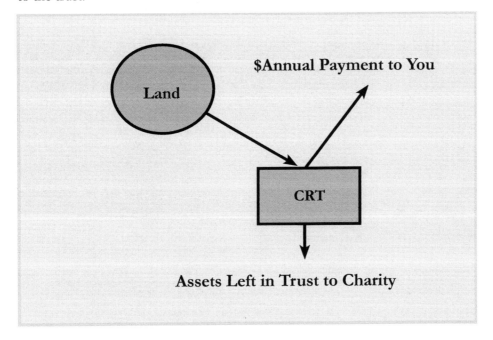

The trust can sell the land without having to pay capital gains tax on the sale. They created the CRT so that it would provide income to them for as long as any one of them is alive, and then to pay the remainder of the trust assets to the college where they met. They take an immediate income tax deduction for the estimated value of the amount the college will get later, and they get income annually from the trust. They may have to pay some tax on the income they receive from the trust, but often it is not as much as they would have had to pay upfront if they had just sold the land. And, last but not least, the value of the land is no longer in their estates, so there won't be any estate tax assessed on that value.

Charitable Lead Trust

Another type of charitable trust is a charitable lead trust ("CLT"). With a CLT, you transfer property to a trust that then pays an annual income ("the lead") to a charity. When the trust terminates after a specified number of years, the remaining assets left in the trust go to a person or persons you name, such as your children. Generally, you won't get an income tax deduction for giving any property to a CLT, but you won't pay any gift tax on the transfer and you have removed some of the value of the asset from your estate. A CLT can be a good choice for an asset that is expected to appreciate in the future, so that the appreciated value won't be in your estate.

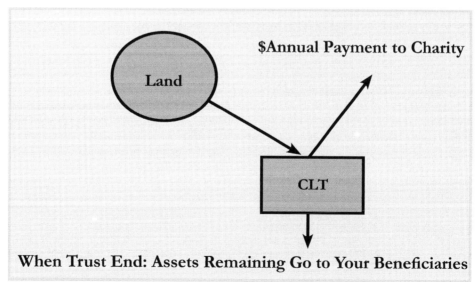

When Trust End: Assets Remaining Go to Your Beneficiaries

Another example: Assume that Norm and Marian in the example above have land that they expect to be worth much more in the coming years as the area around the land is developed. They decide to establish a charitable lead trust that in five years will begin to pay a percentage of the trust assets to their favorite charity. When the trust is terminated in fifteen years, the assets remaining in the trust will go to their grandchildren. There may be a taxable gift to the grandchildren depending on the estimated value of what will pass to them, but that estimated value will be based on the value of the land now, and not the high appreciation expected in the near future. Norm and Marian have removed the value of the asset from their estate, provided for their favorite charity, and assured that the land as it appreciates will benefit their grandchildren in the future.

Other Ways to Reduce Estate Taxes

Federal estate tax can be reduced through a variety of other legitimate estate planning techniques. Since the "coupon" has increased to $5.12 million per person, those with large estates over this amount could benefit from considering some of the methods listed below to reduce potential estate tax liability. The advantages and disadvantages of these techniques vary greatly depending on the individual circumstances of the persons using them. That is why having an experienced attorney or tax advisor can be beneficial in helping you to consider how these techniques might fit your particular situation.

Lifetime Gifts

Under federal tax law, some gifts incur no gift tax, don't require filing of a gift tax return, and don't even use up any of your "coupon." For example, in 2012 you may make an annual tax exempt gift to any one person provided the total amount of gifts to that person during the calendar year does not exceed $13,000. This exemption applies to each person making a gift which means that if both you and your spouse utilize this estate planning tool, you could collectively reduce your estate by giving away $26,000 a year to any number of beneficiaries, free of any federal gift tax. The annual exemption amount changes based on inflation, but over a period of several years the amount of money that you and your spouse (or partner) could transfer to your intended beneficiaries under this method could be quite substantial.

You can also make tax-free gifts by paying someone's medical expenses or tuition bills provided that you pay the bill directly to the medical or educational institution. Gifts of this type are not subject to the annual exemption limits and can be in any amount.

Capital Gains

Making lifetime gifts as described above removes the gifted assets from your estate, potentially reducing the amount your estate would otherwise have to pay in federal estate tax. However, during most years, lifetime gifts may be less advantageous than inheritances when we consider the effect of capital gains taxes. Capital gain is the amount you get when you sell the asset minus your basis. Broadly speaking, basis is the amount you have invested in the asset. So, if you sell an asset for $100 where your basis was $10, you will have a capital gain of $90 that is subject to capital gains tax. When you make a gift during your lifetime, the recipient of the gift has the same basis in the gifted asset as you have. As a result, the $100 asset will have the same $90 capital gain when the recipient sells it as you would have incurred if you had sold it. The transfer of the initial $10 basis to the recipient in this manner is referred to as a "carry-over basis".

However, in most years if you leave the asset as an inheritance rather than a lifetime gift, your recipient now gets a "stepped up basis" to the value of the asset on the date that you died. In the case of our $100 asset, if the value was $100 when you died, the recipient would now have a basis of $100 (rather than a carry-over basis of $10). If the recipient sells the asset for $100, there will be no capital gains subject to tax. Since capital gains taxes are currently around 15%, gifting the asset would have cost the recipient $13.50 in capital gains tax ($90 x .15) while inheriting the asset wouldn't have incurred any tax. This difference in basis is why it is important to consult a tax advisor before making significant lifetime gifts as part of your estate planning.

Note: The law currently provides that there is no automatic "stepped up" basis for property inherited in 2010. Instead, a new "coupon" was introduced in

2010 that allowed the estate to allocate up to $1.3 million in stepped up basis to property left to a non-spouse and an additional $3 million in stepped up basis for property left to a spouse. This law only applied to the estates of people who died in 2010 and was set to expire in 2011. However, as a result of the Tax Relief, Unemployment Insurance Reauthorization, and Job Creation Act of 2010, federal estate tax returned in 2011 and with it, stepped up basis. The new law also offers the executors of an estate of a person who died in 2010 the option of using the 2010 or 2011 rules. That means the executors can elect between (i) a "no federal estate tax" scenario with a carry-over basis or (ii) a federal estate tax exemption of $5 million with stepped up basis. Since this decision affects the capital gains tax and federal estate tax position of you and/ or your designated beneficiaries, it's a decision best made with the advice of your tax advisor.

Let's consider an example applying the law as it stood in 2010 only. Assume Norm dies in 2010 leaving all his property to his 3 children. Also assume Norm's entire estate consists of nine apartment houses each worth $1 million dollars. Finally, let's assume that Norm's original basis in each apartment house was $200,000 or a total of $1.8 million in original basis for the total estate. With the 2010 step up at his death, when Norm's assets are sold by his estate or later by any of his children, those assets will have a total basis of $3.1 million, which is the original $1.8 million basis plus the $1.3 million added at his death. If Norm's estate sells all of the apartment houses for $1 million each before distributing the proceeds to Norm's children, those sales would result in capital gains tax being charged on $5.9 million, which is the difference between the value of the assets ($9 million) and the new basis in those assets ($3.1 million).

If Norm's estate doesn't sell all the apartment houses but instead transfers them directly to his 3 children, each child would receive 3 apartment houses. While none of his children would have to pay capital gains tax when the inheritance is received, each child would have a basis equal to one-third of the $3.1 million new basis, or $1,033,333. Since the original basis in the apartment houses was the same for each house, the new basis is now $344,444, which is one third of $1,033,333. When a child sells an apartment house, he or she must pay capital gains tax on the difference between the total sales price and the new basis of $344,444**.

Now assume that Norm left his estate to his wife Marian rather than his children. Now the assets receive an additional $3 million in basis, making the new basis in the entire estate a total of $6.1 million ($1.8 million original basis plus $1.3 million estate step-up plus $3 million in new basis for spouse only). If Norm's estate sells all of the apartment houses for $1 million each before distributing the proceeds to Marian, those sales would result in capital gains tax on $2.9 million, which is the difference between the value of the assets ($9 million) and the new basis in those assets ($6.1 million). If the estate doesn't sell the apartment houses and instead transfers them to Marian, Marian will have a basis in each apartment of $677,777 ($6.1 million divided by 9 houses).

Based on these examples, you can see the benefit of getting tax advice.

** Note: This example assumes that each apartment house has the same original basis. If the original basis is different for each asset, the new basis will also be different for each asset, as the new basis is the proportional share of stepped up basis plus the original basis.

Irrevocable Life Insurance Trusts

An irrevocable life insurance trust creates a trust that is used exclusively to own life insurance. The trust purchases life insurance on your life, and you make gifts to the trust to pay the premiums. The trust may not be revoked and once you place funds into the trust, they cannot be taken back. Upon your death, the life insurance payout is distributed according to the terms of the trust. Because you do not control the life insurance, it is not considered part of your taxable estate and thus no federal estate taxes are due when the payout is made.

Family Limited Partnerships

A family limited partnership helps families transfer ownership of their closely-held businesses to the next generation of business managers. A family limited partnership, or FLP, is created to hold and manage assets. You may transfer those assets to the FLP in exchange for your interest in the partnership. You then gift some of your partnership interest to your children, perhaps over a number of years. FLPs can save estate taxes in two ways. First, they can remove from your estate now assets that are likely to appreciate. Even though the asset is removed from the estate, you may retain control over the partnership and therefore have continued control over how the asset is managed. Second, the percentage gift you make to an FLP may be valued at less than the same percentage of the value of the assets in the partnership.

For example, assume you establish a partnership with three pieces of real estate each valued at $500,000. The value of the assets in the partnership total $1,500,000. Then you gift a ten percent interest in the partnership to your son. While ten percent of the value of the partnership assets is $150,000 ($1,500,000 x .10), the value of a ten percent interest in the partnership may be appreciably less than $150,000. This is because as a ten percent owner your son doesn't have control over the assets and there isn't likely to be someone willing to pay him $150,000 for the chance to be a minority partner that lacks control. The real value of the ten percent partnership interest depends on many factors, which is why you must be prepared to get a qualified appraisal on the gift when you use an FLP in your planning.

Special Use Real Estate Valuation

Generally, real estate you transfer by way of gift or estate is valued based on the assumption that the real estate will be sold for its "highest and best use" value. For example, farmland may be worth much more if it was sold for residential development than as agricultural land.

However, you or your estate may be able to claim that the real estate should be valued based on its "actual use" rather than the "highest and best use." This can result in significant tax savings, especially if your family intends to continue using the land as farmland rather than selling it to a developer. Special use valuation is complicated and generally requires the assistance of an experienced attorney.

Conclusion

Estate taxes and estate tax planning are a complicated area of the law. If you have an estate greater than a million dollars or have other special circumstances, we recommend that you seek professional advice before employing any of the tax reduction strategies outlined in this chapter..

Important Note

Taxation can all too often present a big challenge to anyone preparing an estate plan. If your estate is large or complex it is recommended that you seek professional tax advice. You should consider hiring a tax expert, either a lawyer or an accountant or even both.

FINALIZING YOUR PLAN

Chapter Overview

This chapter concludes our brief look at estate planning. We review the information, tactics and suggestions provided in this book.

Chapter

11

CHAPTER 11

FINALIZING YOUR PLAN

Deciding What Should Be in Your Estate Plan

Now that you clearly understand the need for an estate plan, it is time to bring together all of the pieces of the puzzle and create your plan. The types of estate planning tools that you use in your estate plan are largely dependent on your situation in life, your religious and philosophical views, and how you wish to distribute your assets. In most cases, assuming that your estate is not complex, you will most likely need only four or five documents to adequately prepare your estate. In order to complete these documents, you will need to consider your situation carefully and make important decisions in terms of what you want for the future.

We discuss some of these considerations briefly below.

Management of Your Property and Finances During Incapacity

One of the first issues that you will need to consider is whether you would like someone to manage your affairs during any period in which you are incapacitated or otherwise unable to do so yourself. Assuming that you make a positive decision in this respect, you will need to consider who would be best placed to act as your agent in the management of your property and finances. You will also need to consider whether any limitations should be placed on the scope of that person's authority.

Once you have determined what you want, the next step will be to create a durable power of attorney for finances and property.

Making Healthcare Decisions During Incapacity

In addition to having someone manage your financial affairs during a period of incapacity, you should also consider appointing one or more persons to make medical decisions for you during such a time. This appointment will be made under a healthcare power of attorney.

You should also consider whether you would like to set out any wishes in a living will regarding the end-of-life treatment that you would or would not like to receive should you ever find yourself in a state of permanent unconsciousness or suffering from a terminal illness. While some people find these decisions particularly difficult, they are nevertheless part and parcel of life and should be given due consideration as part of your overall estate plan.

Appoint Guardians for Your Children

If you have any children, you will need to consider who is best placed to care for them and manage their assets in your absence. Once you have determined who this person is or who these people are, as the case may be, you should ensure that you appoint them as guardians and property guardians of your children under the terms of your will. Remember to check with them first that they are willing to take on the role.

Assemble a List of Your Assets and Liabilities

When considering how you would like to deal with the distribution of your assets following your death, the first thing that you will need to do is to prepare an inventory of your assets and liabilities setting out the current net worth of each asset. This will enable you do determine the net value of your estate and therefore whether it falls within the scope of charges to estate tax.

If your estate is above the current tax threshold for estate tax, you will need to consider the use of methods to reduce your estate tax liabilities. These methods are set out in the preceding chapter.

Your list of assets will also assist you in determining what assets you have to give away, to whom you would like to give them to and how you would like to give them away.

If the value of your assets is such that probate will be required, you should consider the use of a revocable living trust to help reduce the related probate fees.

In addition, the list should also help you determine what assets will need to be transferred into your revocable living trust and what assets you wish to leave under your will. Furthermore, it can be used to identify which accounts and policies should have the beneficiary designations changed so their proceeds and assets (in the case of broker accounts) will be distributed in accordance with your overall estate plan.

Decide Who Will Receive Your Assets

In conjunction with the preparation of your inventory of assets and liabilities, you can decide who you would like to give your assets to and who should receive those assets if the intended beneficiary passes away before you do or refuses the gift. Of course, you are generally free to leave your assets to anyone you choose. The major exception to this general rule relates to spouses. In all states, spouses have a legal entitlement to a fraction of their spouse's estate. In the absence of a spouse waiving this entitlement, you will need to make provision for them in your estate plan.

Decide How and When Your Beneficiaries Will Receive Your Assets

There are three principal ways in which you can leave assets to someone on your death namely under a will, a living trust and by means of one of the non-probate transfer mechanisms referred to in chapter 8. In using these methods, you can choose to leave your gifts directly to the beneficiary or to a trustee, custodian or property guardian (for ease, we'll call each a 'trustee' in this section) who will manage the gift on behalf of the beneficiary until they reach a certain age.

In deciding whether to make a gift to beneficiary outright or to a trustee on their behalf, you will need to consider the age, health and position in life of each of the proposed beneficiaries. If the gift is to a minor, it is wise to leave it in the care of a trustee. If you choose to do this, you will then need to consider whether you should establish a trust of your own either under your will or living trust or whether you simply utilize the trust provisions under your state's

Uniform Transfers to Minors Act (UTMA). Alternatively, you could simply leave the assets to their guardian who will determine how best to manage the proceeds on their behalf.

Similarly, if you have decided to make a gift to an incapacitated person, you will need to consider how that gift will be managed on their behalf. It may well be the case that the person in question has a guardian or agent who can manage that gift but, if not, you may wish to consider setting up a trust fund for them. Where trust funds are established, you will need to determine how long it should continue for and what will happen the assets in the trust fund if the intended beneficiary dies before they receive the benefit of the trust. In this respect, you should consider nominating alternate beneficiaries unless you want the assets to be passed to the person or persons entitled to the residuary estate.

Choosing People to Be in Charge

Apart from leaving your assets to loved ones after you pass, estate planning is fundamentally about choosing the right people to deal with your affairs when you are unable to do so or no longer around to do so. If follows, therefore, that in putting an estate plan together you need to carefully select people to act as executors, successor trustees, trustees, guardians, healthcare agents, agents under a power of attorney and agents under a living will. The selection of the right people will be fundamental to the overall success of your estate plan. We mention in this book a number of different attributes that you should look for in selecting these people and you should refer to these in making your decisions.

When to Do-It-Yourself and When to Include Lawyers

The next step is to decide whether you need to visit your attorney or whether you wish to prepare an estate plan yourself.

Both have their own unique advantages.

Your attorney should be able to advise you as to how you can best accomplish your objectives. He or she may force you to think about the choices that you have made or may even present you with better alternatives. Engaging an attorney to review your personal situation and assist with the preparation of an estate plan is often the best way to ensure that the goals set out in your estate plan are achieved. However, the legal fees incurred in the preparation of an estate plan can be quite significant. It is for this reason alone that many people decide to prepare their own estate plans using books such as this one.

In reality, unless your estate or situation is complex (i.e. it consists of complicated asset ownership structures or has potential estate tax exposures), there is no real reason why you cannot prepare your own estate planning documents. This is particularly so if you wish to keep matters straight-forward and easily understood. If this is so, there is no reason why you cannot prepare your own will, living trust, power of attorney, living will, etc. All that is necessary is a little diligent research into the laws applicable in your state. And with the assistance of this book, and some of the other products from the Enodare estate planning range, there is no reason why you cannot confidently deal with these matters yourself. However, if you do not feel comfortable making your own estate plan, it is best that you contact an attorney.

Important Note

If you decide to prepare your own estate planning documents, we recommend using Will Writer, Enodare's estate planning software. Enodare's unique software will, through a question and answer process, guide you through the process of preparing a variety of estate planning documents including wills, living trusts, powers of attorneys, living wills and more. To learn more about this software, see the information pages at the back of this book or visit www.enodare.com or www.global-wills.com.

Storing Your Documents

Once you have prepared your documents, you will need to consider how and where you should store them. While there are a number of options available to you the principal requirement is that you store them in a safe and accessible place where they can be accessed when needed.

In fact, when it comes to storing legal documents, many people's first choice is to use a safe deposit box. While this is a logical choice when it comes to safety, it's not always practical. In many states if the box is registered solely in your name then, on your death, it will be automatically sealed and your family will need to obtain a court order to open it and remove it contents – that's if they know about it at all. Similar problems arise in times of incapacity. Again, your family may not be in a position to access your living trust, power of attorney or living will documents.

For the aforementioned reasons, it may be useful to consider having a safe deposit registered in the joint names of you and someone else. This someone else can be a spouse or indeed an executor, successor trustee or agent under a power of attorney or AMD. At least, in this way, someone will be able to access the safe deposit box both in times of your incapacity and on your death.

If the idea of registering a safe deposit box in joint names doesn't appeal to you for privacy or other reasons, there are a number of other options available to you. The key criteria will be safety. Make sure to choose a location where the documents will be protected from both fire and flooding. Ideally, you could use a personal safe located either at home or in your office. Always ensure that someone knows the location of your safe and indeed the fact that the documents have been placed in it. Be sure, however, to consider the privacy and security issues associated with letting a person know the combination of your safe or indeed details of how they can find out that combination.

Alternatively, you could consider asking your attorney to store your documents for safekeeping or you could just keep them in a safe place in your home. The choice is yours. Wherever you decide to keep them, it is a good practice to keep copies of these documents where they can be located so that your estate plan can be recreated if it ever needs to be.

Important Note

We also recommend that you use the online storage facilities such as those offered by Legal Vaults™. Legal Vaults™ is a relatively unique service that allows people to store estate planning, medical and other important documents and information online. The information and documents can be accessed in whole or in part by people to whom you have provided the security codes. The use of this highly recommended service ensures that your documents are always to hand when needed. For further information on Legal Vaults™ visit www.legalvaults.com.

Updating Your Estate Plan

It's important to update your estate plan fairly regularly. In fact, we recommend that you update it at least every two to three years or whenever there is a fairly significant change in your personal circumstances. By significant change, we mean the occurrence of events such as marriage, divorce, the birth of a child, adoption or a relevant change in either state law or tax law. You should also consider updating your plan where there has been a significant change to your financial position.

Over time, you will probably change your mind as to whom you wish your assets to pass. At times, the beneficiaries under your estate plan may predecease you as indeed might your executors and trustees, or you may dispose of assets and acquire new ones. All these matters should force you to reconsider the terms of your estate plan and, in particular, whether the estate plan needs to be updated.

In addition, as most states afford spouses a right to claim a particular share of their spouse's estate, a material change in your financial position could result in your estate plan no longer meeting those requirements. As such, you will need to re-visit the provisions of your estate plan to ensure that state law does not intervene to determine how your assets are distributed. This of course might result in the unfortunate circumstance that some of your named beneficiaries might not receive the assets you wished to gift to them.

Every time you update your estate plan you should consider your overall objective and then each aspect of your plan to ensure that it meets that overall objective. Maybe you would prefer to name new executor or healthcare agents? Maybe minor beneficiaries have now grown up and the use of trusts is no longer appropriate? Maybe your adult children have difficulty managing money and it is more prudent to place their inheritance under the management of a trustee rather than giving it to them outright? Be sure that you carefully consider your whole plan and not just part of it – remember every aspect of it interacts with another part!

Finally....

We wish you well in preparing your estate plan. For further information and tools to assist you in the preparation of your plan, we recommend that you visit www.enodare.com or www.global-wills.com.

APPENDIX:

ESTATE PLANNING
WORKSHEET

Downloadable Forms

Blank copies of this form are available to download from our website.

Web: http://www.enodare.com/downloadarea/

Unlock Code: QRP20150

enodare

Appendix

APPENDIX - ESTATE PLANNING WORKSHEET

ESTATE PLANNING WORKSHEET

Before you begin the process of making a will or a living trust, we recommend that you print out this worksheet and complete it as appropriate. It will help you to work out what assets you actually own, and identify your liabilities, before deciding who you would like to make gifts to and how. By having all the relevant details at your fingertips it will save a considerable amount of time in the preparation of your estate planning documents.

The document is also useful for documenting your choice of fiduciaries such as executors, successor trustees, healthcare agents etc.

In addition, by keeping this worksheet with your will and other personal papers, it will greatly assist your executor in identifying and locating your assets and liabilities when the time comes.

Personal Information	You	Your Spouse
Full Name:		
Birth Date:		
Social Security Number:		
Occupation:		
Work Telephone:		
Work Fax:		
Mobile/Pager:		
Email Address:		
Home Address (Include County):		
Home Telephone:		
Home Fax:		
Date and Place of Marriage:		
Maiden Name of Spouse:		

If either of you were previously married, list the dates of prior marriage, name of previous spouse, names of living children from prior marriage(s), and state whether marriage ended by death or divorce:		
Location of Safe Deposit Box (if any):		

Notification of Death (On my death, please notify the following persons)

Full Name	Telephone	Address

Children (Living)

Full Name	Address (If child does not reside with you)	Birth Date

Children (Deceased)

Full Name		

Grandchildren

Full Name	Address	Birth Date

Parents

Full Name	Address	Telephone Number

Brothers and Sisters

Full Name	Address	Telephone Number

Assets

Description & Location	Current Fair Market Value	How is Title Held?*
Real Estate		
Closely Held Companies, Businesses, Partnerships etc.		
Bank Accounts (not IRAs and Retirement Plans)		
Stocks, Bonds and Mutual Funds (not IRAs and Retirement Plans)		

Automobiles, Boats, etc		
Other Property		
Total		

*If you know the property is your separate property, your wife's separate property or community property, so state. If not, state the name(s) that appear on the title, if known, and state whether the property is held with right of survivorship, if known

Liabilities

Description		Amount
Mortgages		
Loans		
Debts		

Other Liabilities		
Total		

Life Insurance and Annuities

Company	Insured	Beneficiary(ies)	Face Amount	Cash Value
Total				

IRAs, 401(k)s and Other Retirement Plans

Company Custodian	Participant	Type of Plan	Vested Amount	Death Benefit
Total				

Distribution Plan
(Describe in general terms how you wish to leave your property at death)

Other Beneficiaries
(Information about persons other than your spouse and family members who you wish to benefit)

Full Name	Age	Address	Relationship

Fiduciaries

(List name, address and home telephone for each person)

	Full Name	Address	Telephone Number
Last Will and Testament			
Primary Executor:			
First Alternate Executor:			
Second Alternate Executor:			
Primary Trustee:			
First Alternate Trustee:			
Second Alternate Trustee:			
Guardian of Minor Children:			
First Alternate Guardian:			
Second Alternate Guardian:			
Living Trust			
Successor Trustee:			
First Alternate Successor Trustee:			
Second Alternate Successor Trustee:			
Agent under a Power of Attorney for Finance and Property			
Agent:			
First Alternate Agent:			
Second Alternate Agent:			

Agent under a Healthcare Power of Attorney			
Healthcare Agent:			
First Alternate Healthcare Agent:			
Second Alternate Healthcare Agent:			

Living Will			
Healthcare Agent:			
First Alternate Healthcare Agent:			
Second Alternate Healthcare Agent:			

Advisors
(List name, address and home telephone for each person)

	Full Name	Address	Telephone Number
Attorney:			
Accountant:			
Financial Advisor:			
Stockbroker:			
Insurance Agent:			
Other Information:			

Document Locations

Description	Location	Other Information
Last Will & Testament:		
Living Trust Agreement:		
Living Will:		
Healthcare Power of Attorney:		

Power of Attorney for Finance and Property:		
Title Deeds:		
Leases:		
Share Certificates:		
Mortgage Documents:		
Birth Certificate:		
Marriage Certificate:		
Divorce Decree:		
Donor Cards:		
Other Documents:		

Funeral Plan

(Describe in general terms what funeral and burial arrangements you would like to have)

INDEX

S

Other Great Books from Enodare's Estate Planning Series

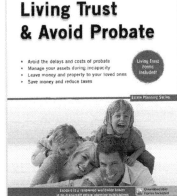

Make Your Own Last Will & Testament

Make Your Own Living Trust & Avoid Probate

Make Your Own Living Will

By making a will, you can provide for the distribution of your assets to your love ones, appoint guardians to care for your children, provide for the management of gifts to young adults and children, specify how your debts are to be paid following your death, make funeral arrangements and much more.

This book will guide you through the entire process of making a will. It contains all the forms that you will need to make a valid legal will, simply and easily.

Living trusts are used to distribute a person's assets after they die in a manner that avoids the costs, delays and publicity of probate. They also cater for the management of property during periods of incapacity.

This book will guide you step-by-step through the process of creating your very own living trust, transferring assets to your living trust and subsequently managing those assets.

All relevant forms are included.

Do you want a say in what life sustaining medical treatments you receive during periods in which you are incapacitated and either in a permanent state of unconsciousness or suffering from a terminal illness? Well if so, you must have a living will!

This book will introduce you to living wills, the types of medical procedures that they cover, the matters that you need to consider when making them and, of course, provide you with all the relevant forms you need to make your own living will!

Other Great Books from Enodare's Estate Planning Series

Make Your Own Medical & Financial Powers of Attorney

The importance of having powers of attorney is often underappreciated. They allow people you trust to manage your property and financial affairs during periods in which you are incapacitated; as well as make medical decisions on your behalf based on the instructions in your power of attorney document. This ensures that your affairs don't go unmanaged and you don't receive any unwanted medical treatments.

This book provides all the necessary documents and step-by-step instructions to make a power of attorney to cover virtually any situation!

How to Probate an Estate - A Step-By-Step Guide for Executors

This book is essential reading for anyone contemplating acting as an executor of someone's estate!

Learn about the various stages of probate and what an executor needs to do at each stage to successfully navigate his way through to closing the estate and distributing the deceased's assets.

You will learn how an executor initiates probate, locates and manages assets, deals with debt and taxes, distributes assets, and much more. This is a fantastic step-by-step guide through the entire process!

Funeral Planning Basics - A Step-By-Step Guide to Funeral Planning

Through proper funeral planning, you can ensure that your loved ones are not confronted with the unnecessary burden of having to plan a funeral at a time which is already very traumatic for them.

This book will introduce you to issues such as organ donations, purchasing caskets, cremation, burial, purchasing grave plots, organization of funeral services, legal and financial issues, costs of pre-arranging a funeral, how to save money on funerals, how to finance funerals and much more.

Will Writer - Estate Planning Software
Everything You Need to Create Your Estate Plan

Product Description

Enodare's Estate Planning Software helps you create wills, living trusts, living wills, powers of attorney and more from the comfort of your own home and without the staggering legal fees!

Through the use of a simple question and answer process, we'll guide you step-by-step through the process of preparing your chosen document. It only takes a few minutes of your time and comprehensive help and information is available at every stage of the process.

The documents are valid in all states except Louisiana.

Product Features:

 Last Wills

Make gifts to your family, friends and charities, make funeral arrangements, appoint executors, appoint guardians to care for your minor children, make property management arrangements for young beneficiaries, release people from debts, and much more.

 Living Trusts

Make gifts to your family and friends, make property management arrangements for young beneficiaries, transfer assets tax efficiently with AB Trusts, and much more.

 Living Wills

Instruct doctors as to your choices regarding the receipt or non-receipt of medical treatments designed to prolong your life.

www.enodare.com

<u>Healthcare Power of Attorney</u>

Appoint someone you trust to make medical decisions for you if you become mentally incapacitated.

 ### <u>Power of Attorney for Finance and Property</u>

Appoint someone you trust to manage your financial affairs if you become mentally incapacitated, or if you are unable to do so for any reason.

 ### <u>And More.........</u>

Enodare's Will Writer software also includes documents such as self proving Affidavits, Deeds of Assignment, Certifications of Trust, Estate Planning Worksheet, Revocation forms and more.

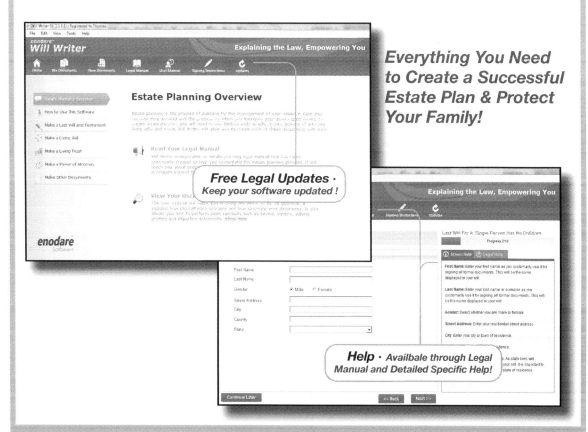

www.enodare.com

Made in the USA
Lexington, KY
15 June 2012